THE

CHRISTIAN DOCTRINE

OF

FORGIVENESS OF SIN;

An Essay.

BY

JAMES FREEMAN CLARKE.

THIRD EDITION.

WIPF & STOCK · Eugene, Oregon

Wipf and Stock Publishers
199 W 8th Ave, Suite 3
Eugene, OR 97401

The Christian Doctrine of Forgiveness of Sin
An Essay
By Clarke, James Freeman
Softcover ISBN-13: 978-1-6667-0496-9
Hardcover ISBN-13: 978-1-6667-0497-6
eBook ISBN-13: 978-1-6667-0498-3
Publication date 3/9/2021
Previously published by
American Unitarian Association, 1870

This edition is a scanned facsimile of
the original edition published in 1870.

CONTENTS.

PART I.—STATE OF THE QUESTION

SECT		PAGE
1	Importance of the Doctrine of Forgiveness	9
2	Taught by Jesus in the Gospels	10
3	And in the Book of Acts	11
4	And in the Epistles of Paul	13
5	And by the other Apostles	15
6	It is necessary for Peace and Progress	17
7	The Moral Law by itself may make men worse, therefore Forgiveness is needed	18
8.	But the Doctrine of Forgiveness is attended with Difficulties	21
9	Which are also found in the New Testament	24
10	Which teaches Doctrines apparently opposed to that of Forgiveness	26
11	Such Apparent Contradictions the Token and Evidence of the Presence of Large Truths	30
12	Truths which God has joined together, not to be put asunder	32
13	The Orthodox do not fully teach Retribution	34
14	Nor the Rationalists, Forgiveness	37

PART II — THE NATURE OF FORGIVENESS

SECT		PAGE
15	What is Forgiveness?	41
16	The Consequences of Sin are Twofold	42
17	The First, a Sense of Divine Displeasure	44
18	Which is removed by Forgiveness	45
19	Implying also an Objective Change in the Mind of God	46
20	The Second Consequence of Sin, which is Depravity of Character, is not immediately removed by Forgiveness	48
21	Recapitulation	50
22	This View of Forgiveness satisfies the Sense of Justice	52
23	And the Need of Pardon	54

PART III — FAITH AND WORKS, OR, THE CONDITIONS OF FORGIVENESS

24	Faith, Works, a Forgiving Spirit, Repentance and Confession, the Scripture Conditions of Pardon	58
25	Faith or Works	60
26	The Opposition of Paul and James	61
27	The Distinction between Forgiveness and Justification	64
28	Faith and Knowledge distinguished	65
29	Faith and Belief distinguished	69
30	Faith and Opinion distinguished	72
31	Importance of these Distinctions	73
32	Christian Faith in particular	75
33	Christian Faith as the Condition of Forgiveness	78
34	Works, growing out of Faith, the Condition of Full Salvation	79
35	Mutual Relation of Faith and Works in the Christian Life	81
36	Results of Forgiveness in the Future Life	82
37	Objections to this Doctrine Answered	85

CONTENTS.

PART IV. — OBSTACLES AND HELPS.

SECT		PAGE
38.	Difficulty of believing in Forgiveness	90
39	All Moral Training makes it more difficult	93
40	Christ's Revelation of Pardoning Love alone makes it possible	93
41	The WORK OF GOD in Human Forgiveness	95
42.	The WORK OF CHRIST in Human Forgiveness; First, as a Teacher	98
43	Second, in his Life	101
44	Third, by his Death Principal Texts	102
45	Various Theories concerning the Effect of Christ's Death	106
46	These Theories, matters of Theology, not of Religion	108
47	How the Death of Christ may produce Faith in Forgiving Love	109
48.	As, in fact, it has actually done	112
49	How Christ's Death may have satisfied God	113
50	By communicating Actual Holiness to Man	117
51	The WORK OF MAN in his own Forgiveness	120
52	His Efforts to do Right a Preparation for Forgiveness	122
53	Repentance, and its Relation to Faith	124
54.	Is Faith Man's Work or God's Gift?	125
55.	God and Man concur in every Act of Faith	126
56.	What Man can do, and what he cannot do	127
57	The WORK OF THE CHRISTIAN CHURCH	130
58.	The Twofold Work of the Church in Forgiveness	136

PART V. — RESULTS OF FORGIVENESS.

59.	The NEW LIFE growing out of Forgiven Sin	140
60.	Its Twofold Character, and that of Goodness in general	144
61.	The Christian Life the Synthesis of both kinds of Goodness	149

CONTENTS.

SECT		PAGE
62.	The Evil of cultivating exclusively the Goodness of Effort	151
63	Forgiveness the Practical Solution of the Problem of Evil	155
64	And that of Human Freedom and Divine Providence	157
65	Conclusion	159

NOTE.

THE American Unitarian Association have, with the consent of the author, and in response to a very frequent and earnest request republished this volume, which has for many years been out of print. The cordial reception of this Treatise in the former editions proves that it meets a very general religious want.

PART I.

STATE OF THE QUESTION.

§ 1   Importance of the Doctrine of Forgiveness.

THE doctrine of FORGIVENESS OF SIN occupies an important place in Christian theology. As connected with the doctrine of the Atonement, it has been placed by many theologians in the centre of the Christian system, and has been called the essential doctrine of Christianity. It is prominent in the teachings of Jesus and his apostles. Its influence on the formation of the Christian character is, as I shall hereafter show, great and constant. Yet the subject is attended with difficulties, which past investigation has not wholly removed. On this account, it seems desirable that the doctrine should be examined anew, its difficulties fairly considered, and an attempt made to remove them.

§ 2 Taught by Jesus in the Gospels.

In the Gospels, we find our Saviour frequently speaking of the Forgiveness of Sin. In the Lord's Prayer, we are taught to pray for Forgiveness every day. Sometimes, when healing diseases, Jesus said to the patient, " Thy sins are forgiven thee." One of these occasions occurred near the commencement of his ministry, and is recorded in the second chapter of Matthew and the fifth of Luke. On this occasion, the scribes accused him of blasphemy, saying, " Who can forgive sins but God alone?" But Jesus assured them that he had power to forgive sins, and confirmed his assertion by healing the sick man. In another place (Luke, vii.), we have the remarkable story of the sinful woman, who washed his feet with tears, and anointed them with the ointment. At this time, Jesus not only said to her, " Thy sins are forgiven," but seemed to show that her love was a proof of it. She was not forgiven because she loved, but she loved because she was forgiven.* Another remarkable passage, in relation to this subject, is that in which Jesus says, that "All sins shall be forgiven to men, except that against the Holy Ghost." So also is that in which he gives to his disciples the authority or the power of remitting sins.† The parable of the "Prodigal Son" turns upon Repentance and Forgiveness. The parable of the "Pharisee and the Publican" teaches that humility is a condition of Forgiveness.

§ 3. And in the Book of Acts.

When we turn to the book of Acts, and read the History of the Planting of the Christian Church, we find that Forgiveness of Sins

---

* This appears from the last clause of verse 47, "To whom little is forgiven, the same loveth little." Love is here not the *condition*, but the *effect*, of Forgiveness, — a distinction, as we shall hereafter see, of great moment.

† John, xx. 23.

was always announced by the apostles as one of the great privileges of the Kingdom of Christ. In Peter's first sermon, he tells his hearers to "repent and be baptized," and they "shall receive the *remission of sins*, and the gift of the Holy Ghost." In his next address (recorded in the following chapter), he tells them to "repent and be converted, that *their sins may be blotted out*." In the fifth chapter, we have another address of Peter to the Jewish Sanhedrim, in which he tells them that " God has made Jesus a Prince and Saviour, to give repentance to Israel and *forgiveness of sins*." In the first account we have of the preaching of the gospel to the Gentiles (Acts, x.), Peter teaches Cornelius concerning the facts in the life of Jesus, and about his resurrection; and says, that, "through his name, whosoever believeth in him shall *receive remission of sins*." In the first account which we have of the preaching of Paul (Acts, xiii.) at Antioch, he says, " Be it known unto you therefore, Men and brethren, that through this

STATE OF THE QUESTION. 13

man is preached unto you the *forgiveness of sins.*" In the book of Acts, therefore, it appears that the *Forgiveness of sins* was the first thing offered, both to the Jews and to the Gentiles, as the gift of God to believers.

§ 4. And in the Epistles of Paul.

When we turn to the epistles of Paul,* we find this doctrine made equally prominent in his system of doctrine. It is the main subject of the Epistle to the Romans, and of the Epistle to the Galatians; for *Justification* is but another name for Forgiveness, and the essential idea of Forgiveness is also conveyed by the word Reconciliation. Throughout Paul's other epistles, the Forgiveness of Sin

* Is it not time to stop calling the apostles *Saints*, and to speak of Matthew, Mark, John, and Paul, without degrading them with this Roman Catholic title? We never hear a minister say, "Let us read from the Epistle of *Saint* Paul," or " SAINT Peter," without feeling that a true reverence for those great men ought to show itself by following their own gospel simplicity. *They* called ALL believers " SAINTS," " HOLY ," for all believers were one in Christ, and partaking of his holiness by faith We discard, so far, their own idea of Christianity when we separate them from their brethren by such titles of honor.

is a prominent idea. Thus (Ephes. i. 7), " In whom we have redemption through his blood, *the forgiveness of sins.*" (Ephes. iv. 32) " Be ye kind to one another, tender-hearted, forgiving one another, even as God in Christ (or by Christ) *has forgiven you.*" (Col. i. 14) " In whom we have redemption, even *the forgiveness of sins.*" (Col. ii. 13) " And you, being dead in your sins, hath he made alive with him, *having forgiven you all trespasses.*" So (Col. iii. 13), too, he tells them to forgive one another, even as Christ forgave them. We see, therefore, from such passages, that, while the *hope* of forgiveness was presented by Paul as a leading motive to induce men to become Christians, he also appeals to their *consciousness of being forgiven* as a main motive to induce them to live as Christians. Future forgiveness is a motive to repentance; past forgiveness is a motive to Love. This, we see, corresponds again with the declaration of Jesus, that the woman loved much " because she had been forgiven much."

STATE OF THE QUESTION. 15

§ 5. And by the other Apostles.

The other Apostles, in their writings, lay equal stress upon this doctrine. The author of the Epistle to the Hebrews (whose purpose is to show that the Jew loses nothing of real value when he becomes a Christian) teaches that the essential advantage and meaning of the priesthood and the temple-worship is replaced by something in Christianity which is, in relation to these, like the Substance to the Shadow. Christ therefore, he says, "is our High Priest, to make reconciliation for the sins of the people." " He is our sacrifice (or covenant-offering) for the redemption of our transgression" (Heb. ix. 15); and "the mediator of that new covenant, of which God had said, that in it he would be merciful to the unrighteousness of Israel, and their sins and iniquities would remember no more" (Heb. viii. 12; x. 17). Luther called the Epistle of James "an epistle of straw," because James lays stress on works, and seems to contradict the Pauline doctrine of justification by faith alone. But even James teaches (v. 15) that by the prayer of faith Sins shall be Forgiven. The apostle Peter, as we might suppose from his sermons in the book of Acts, refers to the same doctrine in his epistles. "Christ also," he says (1 Peter, iii. 18), "hath suffered for sins, *that he might bring us to God.*" "God," he says (i. 3), "hath, by his abundant mercy, begotten us again unto a lively hope by the resurrection of Jesus Christ." In the epistles of John, the Doctrine of Forgiveness is quite as prominent. We read (1 John, i. 9) that " If we confess our sins, He is faithful and just to *forgive us our sins.*" (ii. 2) " He is the *propitiation of our sins.*" (ii. 12) " I write unto you, little children, because *your sins are forgiven.*" And (iv. 10) " Herein is Love, not that we loved God, but that he loved us, and sent his Son to be the *propitiation for our sins.*" John also teaches (iv. 19), " We love him because he first loved us," agreeing with Jesus and the apostle Paul in representing Forgiveness as a motive to Christian Love.

§ 6. Necessary to Peace and Progress.

Not only does the importance of this doctrine appear from the prominent place which it occupies in the Christian Scriptures, but also from its necessity for peace and progress. The mind which is weighed down with a sense of sin can have no peace. The mind that is destitute of peace can make no progress. Anxiety and doubt unnerve the will. There must be inward composure, or there can be no moral energy. Every thing which distracts or divides the mind weakens its powers. And, to accomplish any thing well, we must be able to " forget the things behind, and reach out to those before." The man who is looking back with regret at the failure of past enterprises will not engage with energy in new ones. The man who is looking back with remorse at past violations of duty will not fulfil his present duties with that joyful energy which alone does duty well. Accordingly, we find, throughout all Christian experience, that the peace which comes from a conviction of pardoned sin is one of the essential motives to Christian progress.

§ 7. The Moral Law *by itself* may make men worse.

This brings us to a profound truth of human nature, namely, that to enlighten the conscience by the moral law, instead of making man morally better, may often make him worse. We all know that the conscience, when unenlightened or misinformed, may lead to crime; and that men (like the apostle Paul) have "verily thought that they *ought* to" persecute heretics and burn errorists. But the apostle Paul was the first to recognize the fact, which no one since his time has dared to state as plainly as himself, that moral teaching *by itself*, instead of strengthening, may weaken the moral energies. "The law," he says, "is holy, just, and good;" but "though ordained for life, it becomes death" in consequence of human weakness (Rom. vii. 8—13). "Sin," he says, "*takes occasion by the commandment*," and, being dead before the moral law comes, is developed by it, and becomes active. And, still more forcibly, "The *strength* of sin is the law" (1 Cor. xv.). The way in which this takes place is plain. The law (that is, the sight of moral truth) arouses the conscience, and shows us our duty, but does not give us strength to perform it. It produces a disproportion between our moral powers and our moral aims. In order that we may make moral progress, *two* things are necessary, — a new aim, and a new power; a clearer sight of what we ought to be, and stronger motive to induce us to become it. Now, the moral law only fulfils *one* of these conditions. It shows us what we ought to be. We endeavor to obey it, and may succeed to a certain extent, but never wholly; for the moral law demands perfect obedience, and consequently it always leaves us with a sense of failure.

This, of itself, unnerves us. But more than this. It sets before us duties which are opposed to our wishes, and which we do not even try to fulfil. This leaves us not only with a sense of failure, but with a sense of sin, of guilt. But a sense of guilt no one can endure; and, to escape from it, we must stifle the voice of conscience, cease to think of duty, and plunge recklessly into that other kind of satisfaction which comes from the gratification of desire. Consequently, we go further into guilt than we should have done if the conscience had not been enlightened at all. Much more might be added upon this subject; but for our present purpose this must suffice. We see that to awaken the conscience, and to enlighten it by the sight of a high moral standard, is the *first* and essential condition of moral progress. But we see also, that, in order effectually to make progress, a *second* condition must be fulfilled; otherwise, instead of becoming better, one may be made worse. It is absolutely necessary to take the first step, but still more necessary to take the second. And this second step is taken by means of the Doctrine of Forgiveness. The law teaches duty, and awakens conscience. The gospel offers pardon, and creates Love. The first gives us aim; the second, power. The *way* in which this is effected we shall show hereafter.

§ 8. The Doctrine of Forgiveness is attended with difficulties.

But though the Doctrine of Forgiveness is thus prominent in the New Testament, and is thus important for the development of the Christian character, it is attended with difficulties. WHAT IS FORGIVENESS? We know what forgiveness is when predicated of man; but how can we say in any like sense that GOD forgives? When *man* forgives an insult or an injury, we know what it means. It means either that he ceases to be angry with the offender, or that he remits the punishment of the offence, or both. When the executioners who were about to kindle the pile which was to consume the Maid of Orleans asked her forgiveness, they did not mean to ask her *for a remission of punishment,* for they were not exposed to any punishment: they meant to ask that *she should not be offended with them* for what they were compelled to do. But when a condemned criminal asks forgiveness of the executive power, he does not ask that the King or Governor, in whose hand mercy lies, *shall not be angry with him;* for he knows that they entertain no such feeling. He asks for a *remission of the penalty* of his crime. Now, it would seem at first sight that the Deity cannot be expected to forgive the sinner in either of these ways. Not by ceasing to be angry; for he never was angry. Not by remitting the penalty; for the penalty is not an arbitrary infliction, but the natural and necessary consequence of the offence. When God is said to be angry, when his wrath is spoken of, whatever it means, it cannot mean any thing like human passion. Such passion is inconsistent with the essential attributes of Deity; for it implies weakness, suffering, and selfish irritation. But if God's anger be a holy indignation, or the necessary aversion with which a holy nature contemplates sin, then it would appear that this anger cannot cease until the sinner is altogether purified. And if punishment be the natural consequence of sin; if, in the very nature of things, evil conduct must deprave the character, pollute the mind, harden the heart, — how can we expect these consequences to be remitted? Can the wicked be made happy until they be made holy? Can we enjoy an outward Heaven until we have Heaven within us? And must not each man's happiness, here and hereafter, depend upon the precise degree of his moral character and moral attainments? If, then, forgiveness means either the cessation of God's holy indignation against sin, or the remission of the penalty of sin, which is its natural attendant, it would seem that the one kind of forgiveness is forbidden by the nature of

God, and the other by the nature of man; and that, therefore, forgiveness of sin is an impossibility.

§ 9. *The same Difficulties in the New Testament.*

If now we turn to the New Testament, we meet with the same difficulty there. The doctrine of Forgiveness is, as we have seen, plainly taught. But other things are also taught, which seem, at first view, inconsistent with it. We read, indeed, that God loves the sinner; for we are told that his Love for the sinner was the original cause of the coming of Christ, and that the salvation of the sinner was the final cause of Christ's coming. We read that "God reconciles us, when sinners, to Himself;" and "that, when we were sinners, Christ died for us." The joy in Heaven over one sinner who repents, shows the yearning love toward the impenitent, which dwells in heavenly minds. But, on the other hand, we read, in equally plain and distinct language, that the wrath of God *abides* on the impenitent; that "indignation and wrath, tribulation and anguish," come by the righteous judgment of God upon "every soul that doeth evil." A sound criticism must admit, and seek for the meaning of both these classes of texts, and explain away neither. The indignation against the sinner, ascribed to God, must be consistent with his Love for the sinner; and his Love must consist with this Indignation. It must therefore be an aversion, or an estrangement from the sinner, only because of his sin, and only while he continues in sin. But, inasmuch as the sincerely penitent have sin still clinging to them, and are not wholly free from it, the difficulty which remains is this: How can that Reconciliation to God, which is God dwelling in us, and we in him, and by which we become "partakers of the Divine Nature," take place (which is promised in the New Testament, and is implied in forgiveness), so long as we continue to any degree sinners? Though God is not angry with us with the anger of human passion, must he not be and continue estranged from us by the anger of divine holiness, just so far and so long as any degree of sin remains in us? It would seem, therefore, from the Scripture, that the holiness therein ascribed to the Divine Nature must prevent him from being wholly reconciled to man, while man remains to any extent a sinner. But, according to the same Scripture (Rom. v. 10), "We were reconciled to God when enemies." Here, then, we find the same apparent contradiction, or antinomy, in the Scripture which we before found in the nature of the subject itself.

§ 10. Which seems to declare that Forgiveness in either sense is impossible.

We have seen that we know only two kinds of forgiveness, — one of which removes alienation of feeling, and the other removes the external penalty. We have seen, moreover, that the New Testament opposes difficulties to the supposition that God forgives us in the first sense. But it presents still greater difficulties to the supposition that God forgives us by removing the external penalty. The New Testament plainly teaches a fixed and certain Retribution for all; penitent and impenitent; believers and unbelievers; those who are forgiven, and those who are not. We read that "we shall all stand before the judgment-seat of Christ, that every one may receive the things done in his body, according to that he hath done, whether it be good or bad" (2 Cor. v. 10; Rom. xiv. 10— 12). We read that God "will render to every man according to his deeds," and that "every one of us shall give an account of himself to God." We are also taught in one parable (Luke xix. 13) the principle of Retribution; and in another (Matt. xxv. 14) the principle of Accountability.* According to the first, we

* It is often taken for granted that the Parable of the ten Pounds (Luke, xix. 13), and that of the Talents (Matt xxv. 14), convey the same doctrine. But it is evident the one teaches the *Law of Retribution*, and the other the *Law of Accountability*. In the first, the trust committed to each is the same (ten pounds to ten servants); but the improvement of each is different, and the reward different. In the second, the original trust confided to

are rewarded hereafter according to the exact degree in which we have improved the talents, means, opportunities, faculties, of which we are the stewards. According to the other, we are to account according to the different amount and quality of these talents. To whom much has been given, of him will much be required. This Retribution is not arbitrary, but is compared to the most certain and inflexible operations of nature. "Be not deceived; God is not mocked: whatsoever a man *soweth*, that shall he also *reap*. He who *soweth* to the flesh shall of the flesh *reap* corruption; but he that soweth to the spirit, from the spirit shall reap Eternal Life" (Gal. vi. 8). In the book of Revelation (xx. 12, 13) we read that "the books were opened, and every man judged out of the things written in the books, according to their works." It

each is different, but the proportionate gain is the same, and the reward the same. A parable *might* have been constructed which would have included both doctrines, but it would have been too complicated, and Jesus, with his usual wisdom, separated what he had to say, and taught part on one occasion, and the other part on another.

seems, therefore, that Scripture plainly teaches, what we have already seen to be reasonable, that every action, good or evil, brings after it an inevitable consequence. The consequence in the one case is Eternal Life; that is, as I suppose, an elevation and strengthening of the immortal Principle. The good action re-acts upon the character by a fixed law to make it better. It brings an access of faith and love, which qualifies us for higher action and deeper enjoyment. We "sow to the spirit, and of the spirit reap" spiritual or eternal Life. The consequence in the other case is as unerring. The bad action also re-acts upon the character. He who sows to the flesh reaps corruption. Every higher faculty decays. The power of insight is dulled. Love is frozen in the heart. Faith in God, in things unseen, in universal ideas, in the Right, the Good, the Beautiful, dies out of the soul. The Retribution is sure and certain; certain as the law of gravitation. Forgiveness cannot remit this penalty; for what remission of penalty will change the character? Can one who is stained, weakened, defiled by sin, gain any thing by being taken from an outward Hell, and placed in an outward Heaven? He would rather lose thereby; for to such an one Hell is more satisfactory than Heaven.* Just so, the depraved taste of a vulgar mind finds more pleasure in coarse and profane society than in the company of the pure.

§ 11. *Such apparent Contradictions the token of the presence of large Truths.*

We are therefore brought to this conclusion. On the one hand, Reason demands and Scripture teaches a doctrine of Forgiveness; and, on the other, Reason and Scripture deny that Forgiveness is possible in

---

* Which is well illustrated by Swedenborg in one of his memorable relations He states that a person in one of the Hells thought himself unjustly treated, and wished to be in Heaven. Whereupon the angels were allowed to take him up there, to show him his error No sooner was he placed in Heaven than he fell down, writhing with pain and in great agony, which was only relieved by his being taken back " to his own place," when he became comparatively comfortable. We quote from memory

STATE OF THE QUESTION. 31

either of the usual meanings of the term. But such apparent contradictions are everywhere to be found in the domain of Truth, and like paradoxes are constant in the Scripture. Truths, indeed, are never really contradictory to each other; but they seem so because they are antagonist. As the whole movement of the human body is carried on by means of antagonist muscles; as the movement of the planets round the sun is maintained by constant antagonist forces; as the mental and moral constitution of man consists throughout of antagonist faculties, so in the world of Truth we find the same law of Polarity, and God " has set everywhere two against two." It is only by the perception of these antagonisms that any progress is possible in true knowledge. We must see the contradiction before we can find its solution. We must see the Thesis on the one side, and the Antithesis on the other, before we can find the higher Synthesis which includes the two. It is not by ignoring such difficulties, but by distinctly recognizing them, that we make a truly scientific progress. The charge sometimes brought against Scripture, that it furnishes proof-texts for both sides of every question, is in fact its highest praise; for it shows that Scripture is wide and deep as Nature. Nature, too, furnishes proof-texts on both sides of every question. When we meet, therefore, with these apparent contradictions, we are to regard them as locked doors, by which, when we have found their key, we shall have access to a higher plane of thought.

§ 12. Truths which God has joined together, man must not put asunder.

But hitherto it has happened, that, instead of recognizing both sides of the truth in relation to the subject before us, opposing parties in the Church have taken possession each of a single truth, and passed by the other. One party, calling itself Orthodox and Evangelical, has inculcated the doctrine of Forgiveness. Another party, calling itself Rational,

STATE OF THE QUESTION. 33

Liberal, or Spiritual, has inculcated the doctrine of Retribution. The Orthodox have not denied Retribution; but they have neglected and undervalued it. The Liberals, or Rationalists, have not denied Forgiveness, but have undervalued it. In both cases, one doctrine has been understated; and, as a necessary consequence, the other doctrine has been overstated. For it is also true here that man must not put asunder what God has joined together. And when antagonist truths are divorced, each is mutilated. In the old fable of Eros and Anteros, neither the human nor divine brother could thrive alone; and so in the world of Truth, in the world of Knowledge, each truth fades in the absence of its opposite truth. In the moral world, every virtue needs an antagonist virtue for its own perfection. Courage without caution is not courage, but rashness; caution without courage is not caution, but cowardice. Generosity without prudence is not generosity, but extravagance. Humility without self-respect is not humility, but meanness. Self-respect without humility is not self-respect, but pride. So we might go through all the virtues, and show that each, by destroying its antagonist virtue, destroys itself. The same law prevails in the domain of Truth; for this law of symmetry seems universal.

§ 13. The Orthodox do not teach full Retribution.

The party of thinkers in the Christian Church, usually called Orthodox or Evangelical, have, we have said, in their love for the doctrine of Forgiveness, not done adequate justice to the doctrine of Retribution. They have not taught with sufficient emphasis, that saints, no less than sinners, are to give an account of themselves at the day of judgment, and to be rewarded and punished according to their works. The idea conveyed by their teaching is, that a sinner, at the close of an evil life, may be converted (which is true); and that, being converted, all the consequences of his past sins are removed, which nothing in the Scripture confirms. They have taught that repentance, and faith in the Atoning Sacrifice of Christ, will at any time procure for sinner or saint a forgiveness which obliterates all the penalties of evil doing. But such a forgiveness as this is evidently inconsistent with Retribution, and the effect of such a view is dangerous and pernicious. Many men will postpone repentance till the end of life, if they believe that pardon at that time will remove all the consequences of past sin. Such is in fact the case; and the only argument urged by the pulpit against such procrastination is, that one may die suddenly without an opportunity for adequate repentance. The true argument would be, that every hour in which the real work of life is postponed is so much *actually and for ever* LOST. Every moment given to sin receives an immediate and permanent penalty in so much loss of moral Life. But another pernicious result of this false view of forgiveness is seen in the low spiritual condition of the Christian Church. Believing the whole of Salvation to be contained in forgiveness, and forgiveness to be conveyed exclusively by penitence and faith, the Church has occupied itself with these exercises alone, and not carried Christianity into every-day duties, and into all parts of life. Hence we have seen men living like Christians at church and on Sunday, living like Pagans out of church on Monday; praying Christians in their church, covetous Christians in their shop, ill-tempered Christians in their family. Hence we have seen aristocratic churches, and fashionable churches with room only for the rich; Ecclesiastical conventions condemning dancing, but refusing to condemn Slavery; Monuments erected in Christian Cathedrals to soldiers, excellent only for their skill and success in slaughtering their fellow-men. If those who for conscience' sake submit cheerfully to suffering rather than disobey God declare plainly that they believe in a judgment to come, those who do such things as I have spoken of declare as plainly that they believe in none. A few years since, an eminent statesman, who had plunged his country into war with a neighboring state, the object of which was evidently the acquisition of territory, and who had justified this war by most manifest falsehoods, when about to die, was extremely anxious to be baptized; and, this rite having been performed, and having expressed his belief in forgiveness through the Atonement, passed tranquilly out of the world. Neither himself nor his spiritual adviser seems to have felt any anxiety lest the war, for which he was responsible, might have been unnecessary. They evidently thought that this question had far less to do with his preparation for Eternity than that of his baptism. So long as these views of Retribution are held, so long must the standard of character in the Christian Church be low.

§ 14. Nor the Liberalists full Forgiveness.

On the other hand, the party of thinkers in the Church, sometimes called Rational or

Liberal Christians, have not always done adequate justice to the doctrine of Forgiveness. Believing strongly in the moral law, they have maintained correctly the doctrine of Retribution. Believing also in moral freedom, they have taught that each man's destiny depended on the fidelity with which he exercised it. And, believing in the justice of God, it seemed to them impossible that he could remove the consequences of sin, on account of the single act of penitence or faith, and make those who had wrought a single hour equal with those who had borne the burden and heat of the day. They have seen, that, in this world, success depends not upon single efforts, but upon patient continuance in well-doing. They have, therefore, rejected the common doctrine of forgiveness. But, inasmuch as forgiveness of sin is evidently taught in the Bible, they have explained it as meaning this; that, when a man has repented of any course of evil conduct, and has reformed his character so as to be as good a man as he was before, he will be as happy a man as he was before. But this doctrine of forgiveness differs from that of the New Testament in several points. First, it is a future forgiveness, whereas that of the New Testament is present. Secondly, its condition is reformation, or entire change of character; whereas the condition of forgiveness in the New Testament is repentance, or change of purpose, and the act of faith which attends repentance. And, thirdly, this forgiveness is not given by God, but earned by ourselves; and it proceeds, not from the mercy, but the mere justice, of the Deity. The practical evils resulting from this defective view of forgiveness are the reverse of those resulting from defective views of retribution. As the Christian life is weakened by the one in its sense of accountability, so it is weakened by the other in its sense of dependence. The one defect palsies effort; the other weakens love. We need the doctrine of a present forgiveness of sin, to create in the soul a sense of the immediate love of God. We need to feel that God gives us forgiveness now, not that he will give it to us hereafter. We need to be reconciled and made at one with him, before we can have the strength necessary to enable us to work out our salvation. The New Testament motive is not, "Do good *that you may be* forgiven," but "Do good because you *have been* forgiven." "Be kind to one another, tender-hearted, forgiving one another, even *as God in Christ has forgiven you.*" — "Brethren, *if God so loved us,* we ought also to love one another."

We have thus considered the importance of the Doctrine of Forgiveness, and the difficulties which surround it, — difficulties which have caused different parties of thinkers to omit one side or the other of the Divine Law. Let us now pass on to inquire what the true Doctrine of Forgiveness is.

PART II.

THE NATURE OF FORGIVENESS.

§ 15. What is Forgiveness?

HAVING thus considered the importance of the Doctrine of Forgiveness, and the difficulties which attend the doctrine as it is usually taught, we proceed to ask whether these difficulties can be removed. And the first step to be taken is to analyze anew the notion of Forgiveness. What is it? What do we mean by it? What is necessarily included in it? In any controversy or difficult inquiry, a great deal is often gained by a careful analysis of the terms under discussion. Unless this is done, a controversy may be indefinitely protracted, and no step taken toward its final settlement. We often hear discussions of questions like these: — " Was Christ a literal sacrifice?" " Was his death a real expiation of sin?" " Was it an atonement to God?" In such discussions, both sides proceeding to argue, *pro* and *con*, without first defining the meaning of the terms *Expiation, Sacrifice, Atonement*, no practical result is obtained.

§ 16. The Consequences of Sin are twofold.

God's forgiveness of sin, however much it may differ from human forgiveness, must have some analogy with it; for otherwise we could not understand it. We have seen, that, when man forgives man, it is by remitting one or another of the two penalties of the offence; — one of the penalties being anger, or estrangement from the offender; the other penalty being some outward act of punishment, some external suffering or loss inflicted on the offender. Now, this anger on the side of the injured party, and this suffering inflicted in return upon the injurer, are the natural

THE NATURE OF FORGIVENESS.

consequences of the offence committed against man. What are the natural consequences of the offence against God? They are these two: First, a sense of Divine displeasure; and, secondly, a deterioration of the moral character. As far as the sinner himself is concerned, these two are the natural, necessary, and immediate consequences of sin. By a law of his nature, the operation of which we shall look at hereafter, he feels himself under the displeasure of God. Whether God be displeased, or whether he be not displeased, makes no difference so far as this feeling is concerned. This consequence is immediate and inevitable. So, too, of the other. The question of positive punishment hereafter may be omitted, as far as the question of immediate, present forgiveness is concerned. The immediate, outward penalty of sin is the present depravity of character, occasioned by the formation of an evil habit. Now, we ask, are either of these consequences removed by forgiveness?

44 THE NATURE OF FORGIVENESS.

§ 17. The first, a sense of Divine Displeasure

The sense of Divine displeasure, which is an inevitable consequence of every act of wilful sin, is its heaviest penalty. By a law of the conscience, as fixed as the law of gravitation, every wilful transgression produces in the transgressor's mind a sense of Divine displeasure. Just so far as our conscience is awake and active, we feel on such occasions that God, because of his holiness, must regard us with disapprobation. This feeling produces again estrangement on our part. Like Adam, we hide ourselves from God among the trees of the garden; turning from spiritual things to temporal, and trying to forget that God sees us, by looking away from him. This leads us to cast off fear, and restrain prayer; to cease from filial, affectionate communion with our Heavenly Father, and to say with the Centurion, "I am not worthy that thou shouldst come under my roof." This state of mind is described in the New

THE NATURE OF FORGIVENESS. 45

Testament as " estrangement," " alienation," " separation from God," " enmity against God." It is enmity, in the sense of *repugnance*, of a dislike to think of that which gives us pain.

§ 18. Which is removed by Forgiveness.

Now, it is evident from the New Testament, that forgiveness implies the removal of this first and worst consequence of sin. The words everywhere used concerning it are reconciliation, peace with God, being at one with God, dwelling with God, and God with us. A happy, childlike relation of the soul with God, in which all sense of Divine anger is taken away, is immediately given to the Christian believer. In this sense the forgiveness of sin is immediate. " Being reconciled by faith, we have peace with God through our Lord Jesus Christ." " Being no more strangers, but sons, " the spirit is put in our hearts by which we cry, Father." " There is now no condemnation to them which are in

46 THE NATURE OF FORGIVENESS.

Christ Jesus;" and "through him we have access by the spirit to the Father," and have "confidence to come boldly to the mercy-seat for grace to help in time of need." Such peace with God, such joy with God, such filial communion with God, is everywhere spoken of in the New Testament as belonging to forgiven sin.

§ 19. *Implying an objective Change also in the mind of God.*

But if the subjective displeasure of God, that is, the sense of it in the human soul, is thus removed by forgiveness, the objective displeasure, or real feeling of displeasure, in the mind of God, must also be removed. For he could not make us feel that he was reconciled with us, if he were not so. If God communicates to man the conviction of pardon, this is sufficient evidence that there is no alienation from man on the part of God. The difficulty remains, indeed, to explain how God can be fully reconciled, so long as any degree of sin remains in the human being.

THE NATURE OF FORGIVENESS. 47

This difficulty I have not forgotten, and shall attempt its solution hereafter. But it is quite important to distinguish between a fact, and the explanation of that fact. At present we have to do with the fact, and not its explanation. The fact before us is, that there is a forgiveness taught in the New Testament, and confirmed by Christian experience, which removes every thing which separates us from the Divine Love, whether the obstacle be on our part or on the part of the Deity. The proof of this fact is manifest throughout the New Testament, and written in the whole history of Christian experience. This forgiveness, which removes all sense of the Divine displeasure, is an immediate forgiveness. And in this consists essentially the whole meaning and blessing of pardon. Pardon, therefore, is not a formal act of the Divine government, remitting the legal penalty of the offence, but an actual change of relation between the human child and his Heavenly Father. It is a renewal of Fatherly and filial intercourse. It is the expression of love on the side of the Parent; the reception of love on the side of the child.

§ 20. The second, Depravity of character, Forgiveness does not immediately remove

The first consequence of sin, which is separation from God, is therefore removed by forgiveness immediately. The second, depravation of nature, is not removed immediately. There is no evidence in the New Testament that pardon removes directly the vicious habits, the depraved character, the corrupted tastes, the torpor of mind, the infirmity of will, which have resulted from the practice of evil. In the parable of the Prodigal Son, the twofold penalty of sin is represented by the younger son's absence from his Father's house, and the waste of his substance. When he was forgiven, the first consequence of his sin was removed, but not the second. He received from his Father every evidence of a new love. They were re-united in the bonds of a tender affection; but he did not

THE NATURE OF FORGIVENESS. 49

receive again the patrimony which he had wasted. *All that his Father had* was the portion of the elder son; but the younger possessed again his Father's affection, and this was enough. He was willing to be as one of the hired servants. He cheerfully continued to bear the outward penalty which he had brought upon himself by wasting his patrimony.

But, though forgiveness does not remove immediately that depravity of nature which is the secondary consequence of sin, it removes it mediately and indirectly by giving new energy to the moral nature. The sense of pardon creates a power of grateful affection in the heart, which enables it to retrace its steps, rebuild its character, form new habits of virtue, and, forgetting the ignoble past, reach forward to a better future. As it is a law of mechanics, that what we lose in time we may gain in power; so also here, the new power of spiritual life may more than compensate for many a wasted day.

THE NATURE OF FORGIVENESS.

Experience shows that he who has received the conviction of forgiven sin is a new creature. Old things have passed away, and all things have become new.

§ 21. Recapitulations.

Let us recapitulate what we have thus far seen. We have seen that the doctrine of Forgiveness occupied an important place in the Gospels and Epistles, and that it was important for human peace and moral progress, but that there were difficulties connected with it. These difficulties were that forgiveness must either mean, that God ceases to be angry with the sinner, or that he ceases to punish the sinner. The first supposition seemed inconsistent with the moral character of God; for, if by God's anger we understand any thing akin to human passion, that of itself would imply imperfection. Rejecting this supposition, therefore, we must believe the anger of God to be the repugnance with which a holy being necessarily regards sin,

THE NATURE OF FORGIVENESS. 51

and the estrangement of feeling with which a holy being necessarily regards a depraved one. This view, however, of Divine anger creates a new difficulty; for how can this holy displeasure cease, and man be forgiven in this sense, so long as he continues at all infected with the disease of sin? But the best of Christians is, to some degree, a sinner: therefore it would seem that the best of Christians can never be fully reconciled to God. The other view of forgiveness which makes it consist in the remission of the external penalty of suffering and loss, we saw, presented still greater difficulties. For this loss and suffering is not an arbitrary penalty to be inflicted hereafter, but the present, immediate, and natural consequence of each sinful act. Therefore, notwithstanding the difficulty connected with the first view of forgiveness (a difficulty not yet solved), we have concluded that forgiveness means the direct and immediate removal of the alienation existing between the sinner and the Deity. This alienation is both subjective and objective. Subjective, so far as it is a sense of God's displeasure in the sinner's mind, arising from the action of his own conscience, and causing him to turn away from God;—objective, so far as there is any actual alienation in the Divine mind corresponding to it. Forgiveness, we have concluded from the teaching of the New Testament, and from the history of Christian experience, must mean the removal of this alienation, and not the remission of the outward penalty. This penalty is not removed immediately by the act of pardon, but indirectly by means of the moral power created anew in the soul of the forgiven sinner.

§ 22. Our view of Forgiveness satisfies the sense of Justice.

This view of forgiveness completely satisfies both the sense of justice and the need of pardon. The sense of justice is satisfied; for the sinner is not placed by forgiveness exactly where he was before. He still has

THE NATURE OF FORGIVENESS. 53

to bear a portion of the penalty. The law
of retribution holds on its way. Its consequences are not suspended nor annulled.
As he has sown, so he reaps. His position in the moral universe, his moral growth,
power, capacity, is the exact result of his
fidelity to conscience, of his loyalty to duty.
He who by means of his pound has gained
one pound is made ruler over a single city.
He who has gained five pounds is made
ruler over five cities. The man who has
pursued a course of vice through a long
life, and then repents, is *not* made equal
with him who has passed from innocent
childhood through a virtuous youth, and a
manhood whose strength has been devoted
to usefulness. In one respect only are these
two equal; in their nearness to God, and
the sense of his full Fatherly love. But
they differ in outward position, rank, powers of usefulness, capacity to serve their
Master. One is a high Archangel, near
his throne; the other far down, in a lower

rank of the Heavenly Hierarchy. Yet he is happy there; for his cup is full of joy. It is not so large a cup as it would have been, had he been more faithful; but it is full.

§ 23. And the Need of Pardon.

The need of pardon is also satisfied by this view of forgiveness. The prodigal Son was willing to be made as one of the hired servants, provided he could be received again to his Father's house and heart. The penitent sinner, in like manner, accepts willingly the external consequences of his sin, provided he can be at one with God, and have an ever-present sense of his Heavenly Father's love. He is even glad to honor the law which he has outraged, by cheerful submission to its necessary penalties. He sees far above him those Cherubic intelligences, those Seraphs of love, who have been faithful perhaps in their few things, while he has wasted the many gifts with which he was endowed. He has gone down, and they have gone up. His shining light has grown dim; their small candle now blazes like a star in the firmament of God. But he is well content with this low position and small stewardship; amply compensated for this loss of capacity, power, and office, by the conviction that *inwardly* God is as near to him in love as to them. He has perhaps wrought but one hour, and has been made equal with those who have borne the burden and heat of the day, in the full sense of an all-embracing Divine love. So, in an earthly household, when the wilful child comes to himself, and becomes again obedient, he is received with a joy and affection without limit. He has an equal share with all the rest in the family affection; and no one complains that he has it, for the joy of the whole is increased by his return. Thus, while in the vast order of the universe there is rank above rank, heaven above heaven, thrones, dominions, principalities and powers,

THE NATURE OF FORGIVENESS.

> "Spirits and intelligences fair,
> And angels waiting on the Almighty's chair,"—

each, in every part of this order, partakes fully of the Divine life which flows through the whole. Or, to use the image of the apostle, — though "there are many members, there is but one body;" eye and ear and foot, each co-operating in its place for the good of the whole. Each member is satisfied with its place and duty, while it is working for the good of the whole. When the motive is private advantage, there is no content while another stands higher than one's self; but, when the motive is public good, one is content with any position of real usefulness, no matter how humble in appearance; for then the gain of the whole is the gain of the individual. We see the operation of this principle in those associations which are organized for some great work. They have an *esprit de corps*, or corporate spirit, which causes the humblest member to feel himself exalted by the success of the whole. How much more in that great corporation of which Christ is the head, and of which the spirit of God is the pervading life! To the humblest member of this great society, — a society whose members on Earth and in Heaven make one communion, with a common object, — it may be said, "All things are yours;" for you are "heirs of God and joint heirs with Christ." Each pardoned sinner enters into the full communion of this pervading Love; and the liquid element of Love everywhere finds its level. It constitutes the true equality. It breaks down all walls of separation. It brings down the high mountain, and fills up the low valley. No distinctions of rank, power, or greatness, can stay the flow of its tidal wave. For it makes

> "The spirit of the worm beneath the sod
> In love and worship blend itself with God."

PART III.

FAITH AND WORKS; OR, THE CONDITION OF FORGIVENESS.

§ 24. Faith, Works, a Forgiving Spirit, Repentance, and Confession, as Conditions of Pardon.

HAVING thus considered the nature of Forgiveness, we next pass to inquire, "How do we obtain Forgiveness?" The New Testament seems to answer this question in different ways. According to the Apostle Paul, we are justified by FAITH, and by faith alone. According to James, a man is justified by WORKS, and not by faith only. Jesus makes a DISPOSITION ON OUR PART TO FORGIVE, the condition of our being forgiven (Matt. vi. 15; Mark, xi. 26). And in the parable of the unforgiving servant (Matt. viii. 23–35), we find that the forgiveness which had been received was lost again, in consequence of an unforgiving spirit in the servant. REPENTANCE is also evidently made the condition of forgiveness in the parable of the prodigal Son; and in Luke, xxiv. 47, it is connected with the remission of sin, as it is also in Peter's discourses (Acts, ii. 38, and Acts, iii. 19). CONFESSION is elsewhere declared a condition of forgiveness, as in 1 John, i. 9. But, if we carefully consider these passages, we shall find, that, when any one of them is spoken of by itself as a condition of forgiveness, the others are supposed and implied. Thus the repentance of the prodigal Son proceeded not only from a sense of his misery, but from a *faith* in his Father's goodness. "How many hired servants of my Father," he says, "have bread enough and to spare, and I perish with hunger!" His repentance also was not complete till it had shown itself in action and confession; till he had gone to his Father, and confessed to him his sin. So, when *forgiveness of others* is made a condition of being forgiven ourselves, it is evidently as a test of a true penitence and a true faith. And, when confession is made a condition of forgiveness, it is apparent, in like manner, that it is a confession, which, proceeding from penitence and faith, is itself an evidence of their presence. The two duties most difficult to the natural man are to confess his own faults, and to forgive the injuries he has received from others. These, therefore, are made the tests and evidences of true penitence and faith.

§ 25. Faith or Works the Condition?

The only real difficulty, therefore, on this subject, is the question, *Are we forgiven in consequence of faith, or in consequence of works?* On this question the two apostles have been thought to differ, and it has been a subject of repeated and very animated discussion in the Christian Church. But here we see the importance of defining the terms in discussion before the argument be-

THE CONDITIONS OF FORGIVENESS.

gins. Every thing depends on the meaning of the word forgiveness. If the meaning be given which we have ourselves here ascribed to it, namely, the removal of that estrangement or alienation from God, which is one consequence of sin, then the answer is, we are forgiven or justified by faith. But if by forgiveness is meant the removal of that depravity of character which we have seen to be the other consequence of sin, then the answer is, we are justified by works. And if both of these meanings are included in the term justification, then apparently the proper answer would be, that we are justified by both, — by faith and works.

§ 26. The Opposition of Paul and James.

And this is probably the explanation of the apparent opposition between Paul and James. When Paul speaks of *justification*, he means by it simply the taking away of the sense of sin, and the reconciliation of the soul to God. He means to teach that this blessedness of reconciliation comes at once into the soul, as soon as it is able to trust itself to the forgiving love of God. He means to oppose the idea that we must wait before receiving this blessedness, until, by laborious discipline and ascetic culture, we have conquered all sinful habits. His doctrine is, that we are reconciled to God, *that we may* reform our character, and not *because we have* reformed our character. He lays, therefore, this stress on *justification by faith alone*, in order to oppose the error of that false humility which says it is not fit to be forgiven, — of that false conscientiousness, which thinks it has no right to be forgiven, — and the distrust of God, which cannot believe that it will be forgiven till by laborious process it has removed, one by one, every stain inhering in the soul. Paul, therefore, makes Forgiveness the result of Faith alone, but teaches as strongly that this Faith must produce Works, and that out of Forgiveness must proceed Obe-

THE CONDITIONS OF FORGIVENESS. 63

dience. He teaches those whose sins have been forgiven, that they are not yet sure of final salvation, but must "work out their salvation with fear and trembling." In the Epistle to the Romans, he gives a beautiful description of the progress of religious experience in the human soul. In the first two chapters, he describes the Moral Death of Jew and Gentile. In the seventh chapter, he describes the Struggle and Conflict in the mind under the influence of the Law. The fifteenth to the twenty-fourth verses express Despair; the twenty-fifth verse, Peace and Pardon through Faith in Christ. The first part of the eighth chapter describes the Walk in the Spirit; and the last part, Full Redemption and Final Glory. Nothing can be more profound, or more true to human experience, than the whole of this description.

The Apostle James, on the other hand, writing to those who had abused or misunderstood Paul's doctrine, and who thought it enough to *say* they had faith, and whose lives showed no purpose of obedience, argues that justifying faith is a working faith. He asserts that works are the necessary result, *and therefore a part*, of true faith; and that faith is imperfect without them. There may or may not be a formal contradiction between this statement and that of Paul; but it is evident enough that there is no real contradiction. Paul is speaking of the inward experience of forgiven sin; James, of that, and of the life which flows from it. Paul denies that works are necessary to produce justification: James denies that justification can fail of producing them. Paul opposes those who would make works a condition of pardon: James opposes those who think them unnecessary, as the result and evidence of pardon. Each is teaching an important truth, and these truths are antagonist, but are not contradictory.

§ 27. The Distinction between Forgiveness and Justification.

It may here be asked, whether the term justification means the same thing as the term forgiveness. According to Rom. iv. 6–8, it would seem to do so; for Paul there quotes the passage, "Blessed are they whose iniquities are forgiven, and whose sins are covered," as a description of the happiness of one who is justified without works. So far, therefore, as man's feelings are concerned, they are the same; and he who is forgiven is justified. But, though the substantial meaning of these terms is the same, their relative meaning is different. Forgiveness relates to the removal of the sense of guilt and alienation in the human mind. Justification relates to the Divine act, by which it is removed. Two things are implied in the reconciliation of the sinner to God. The first is God's love, which reconciles; the second is the sinner's sense of being reconciled. Justification expresses chiefly the first idea; and forgiveness, the second.

§ 28. Faith and Knowledge.

What, then, is the nature of this faith which is the only condition of Forgiveness?

Faith in general has been defined " A realizing sense of spiritual things," which corresponds nearly to the definition in the Epistle to the Hebrews, "The substance of things hoped for; the evidence of things not seen." It is the organ by which we perceive the Spiritual world. And without this organ we should have no personal evidence of its existence, any more than the blind man has of the existence of color. The blind man may believe that there is such a thing as color, on the testimony of others; and, without the exercise of faith, we may believe, on the testimony of others, in the existence of a spiritual world. But it is faith which gives us personal evidence of its reality, or what may be called a realizing sense of it. We may distinguish between Knowledge, Faith, Belief, and Opinion, in the following way. Knowledge and Faith have the same degree of certainty, and both come from experience: but the object of Knowledge is the external world; the object of Faith, the internal world. The instrument of Knowledge is sensation; the instrument of Faith, intuition. By Knowledge we mean the certainty we have attained of the existence of outward things by the experience of our senses. By Faith we mean the certainty we have obtained of inward things by the experience of our intuitions. Our certainty, therefore, of the existence of the outward and inward world has precisely the same foundation, — that of Experience. Argument, Reasoning, Logic, can neither give nor take away this certainty, in the one case nor in the other. To think to obtain Faith in God by means of argument is as absurd as to think to obtain a knowledge of forms or colors by means of argument. So, too, no argument, however plausible or cogent, can convince a man of the non-existence of what he has seen; and no argument, however logical it may appear, can in the slightest degree shake our assurance of the existence of those spiritual things of which we have taken cognizance by Faith. If it be said that we may be mistaken in our intuitions and misinterpret our consciousness, it is also true that we may be deceived by our senses, and misinterpret their testimony. But, because our senses may deceive us, no one thinks of denying that they are the source of knowledge; and, because our intuitions may deceive us, no one can properly deny that they are a legitimate source of certainty. If we have all of us a greater degree of certainty concerning the outward world than we have concerning the inward world, the reason is simply this, that we have had more experience of the one than of the other. If our intuitions had been as numerous and frequent as our sensations, our certainty of the spiritual world would have been equal to our certainty of the material world. The proof of this is, that, in exact proportion to the exercise of Faith and spiritual insight, increases our assurance of the reality of God, Eternity, Heaven. The mass of men, whose senses are constantly exercised upon the material world, while their souls are seldom exercised upon the spiritual world, look upon the first as real, and the second as unsubstantial. Religious men, who continually contemplate God, Truth, Right, Love, Immortal Beauty, perceive these things to be real; while, to some of them, material things become shadowy and unsubstantial. Jesus, who dwelt by habitual insight in the heavenly world, speaks of spiritual things with the startling distinctness and accuracy of an eye-witness. To him they were evidently quite as real and certain as the things of this world.

§ 29. Faith and Belief

Faith differs from Belief also, but in another way. The object of Faith is reality: the object of Belief is a proposition. Belief comes through Reasoning and Logic; Faith, through Intuition and Insight.* The experi-

* The passage (Romans, x 17) which declares that "Faith comes by hearing, and hearing by the Word of God," is not inconsistent with this assertion. The *objects* of Belief and of Faith are both furnished from without; but there is also an inward

ence of the outward and inward world, which is the source of Knowledge and Faith, being reduced to formal statements by the action of the intellect, becomes the object of Belief. By Faith we perceive the love of God. We reduce this experience to a verbal statement as nearly as we are able, and then it becomes a *Doctrine concerning God's Love*, which we believe. This statement we may communicate to another, who has not had any like experience; and on the strength of our testimony he may believe it also. Then we shall both have the *same creed* or belief, but by no means the *same faith*. In like manner, two persons, having the same religious experience or the same faith, may not represent it to their minds by the same statements. One possessing more analytic power, and a better reasoning faculty, may make a more correct statement than the other of his experience.

action of the mind necessary in each case This *inward* action is, in one case, Reasoning; in the other, Intuition: the outward source is, in both cases, Testimony. The testimony concerning Christ, when reasoned upon, becomes Belief in Christ; when realized by Intuition, becomes Faith in Christ

THE CONDITIONS OF FORGIVENESS. 71

Then they will have the *same faith*, but a *different belief*. And the belief of one will be right; that of the other, wrong.

The difference between Faith and Belief will be made more clear by the following illustration: one man believes that Jesus Christ is God; another believes that he is the Son of God, and subordinate to the Father: but both trust in him as a Saviour, able to save to the utmost; as a Teacher whose word is always truth; as a Friend whose love is the most valuable treasure they possess. The *belief* of these two men is evidently very different. But their *faith* is the same; for each trusts wholly in Jesus. The man who believes that he is subordinate to the Father, trusts *entirely* in him; and the other can do no more. Again, they may differ as to the way in which Christ saves the soul. One may believe that it is by paying a debt due to God, and bearing the penalty of human transgression. The other may believe that it is by manifesting the truth and love of God to the soul, and by creating a new life therein. But, while holding these different beliefs as to the *way* of Salvation, they both are receiving daily peace and strength from communion with their spiritual Friend. Both rely on him practically in the same way, and therefore must have the same faith. Meantime it is evident that two men may hold precisely the same belief, and accept intellectually the same creed; and, while one of them has a strong faith, the other may have no faith at all. For do we not see every day, in all the churches, those who hold strongly to every variety of creed, but who have not attained thereby, as yet, to any Christian faith?

§ 30. Faith and Opinion.

Faith, we have seen, produces *certainty;* Belief, only probability. Still lower down is *Opinion*, which produces neither certainty nor probability, but only a thought. When a subject is presented to us, we have an opinion concerning it, which results from the first impression it makes upon our mind. These opinions are not the result of examination: they are not supported by reason, nor based upon evidence. "Opinion," says Milton, " is knowledge *in the making;* " but, unfortunately, in most cases it remains unmade. Most persons, when they speak of their creed or their belief, mean in reality only their opinions. Their notions on religious subjects are not the result of any careful or conscientious investigation, but of the impressions they have passively received, of the thoughts which they have been accustomed to hear. In order to turn their opinions into belief, it would be necessary to subject each to an examination, and to weigh the arguments for and against it. Only by this process can Opinion be changed into Belief.

§ 31. Importance of these Distinctions.

When Faith is confounded with Belief, many evil results follow, which we see illustrated everywhere in the present condition of the church. Salvation is made to depend on the belief of dogmas, instead of a right state of the affections. For, if a man believes that his creed is his faith, he must necessarily be a Dogmatist. Again, he must be a bigot, and cling to his dogma with an exaggerated fondness, idolize it, worship it, and believe in its infallibility. All which is true when predicated of Faith; namely, that it produces certainty, assurance; that it saves the soul; that without it there is no comfort, hope, nor peace; he will transfer to his dogma and predicate of his Creed. Then follows intolerance as another necessary result of this confusion. All supposed speculative errors he will confound with spiritual deficiencies. What he believes a heresy he will also believe to be irreligion, and to doubt his creed must be to him the same thing as to be without God or hope in the world. It may safely be assumed, that the destruction of the spirit of bigotry, intolerance, and sectarianism in the

THE CONDITIONS OF FORGIVENESS. 75

Christian church, depends upon its recognition of this distinction between Faith and Belief, between Religion and Theology. The man who does not recognize this distinction (in some form or other) ought to be a bigot, and must be one.

§ 32. Christian Faith in particular.

Faith, *in general*, we have seen to be the sight of spiritual things. *Religious* faith is the sight of God in his works and in his providence. *Christian* faith is the sight of God as revealed in Jesus Christ. Thus Faith in general produces spirituality; Faith in God produces religion; Faith in Christ produces the Christian life. God has made a special revelation in Christ, and Christian faith, therefore, is specific; having a character of its own, derived from its object. GOD IN NATURE reveals his power, his wisdom, and his goodness. He reveals himself as the great, wise, and benevolent Order of the Universe. He is above all, through all, and within all.

Above all, as the Creator; through all, as the Sustainer; and within all, by communicating his Life and Joy. God also reveals himself IN THE HUMAN SOUL, by its intuitions of Justice, Truth, Beauty, Personality, Infinity, and Being, — as the personal Moral ONE, sole fair, sole true. But the Revelation in CHRIST has something special in it, not found in God's revelation through nature, or his revelation in the human soul. In Christ He comes to man, estranged from him by sin, to reconcile him again to himself. In Christ he manifests himself, not as Creator, nor as King, but as Father. He enters into a new and beautiful relation with the individual soul, teaching it to cry " FATHER," and to feel itself his Child. We find in nature few, if any, indications of forgiveness. Everywhere in nature we read Law, — inexorable, unrelenting LAW. These Laws, indeed, are always adapted to the good of the whole, and to the advancement and perfection of the race; but beneath them the individual is continually crushed. Nature never pardons. Her wheels thunder on along their iron track, nor turn out to spare any helpless mortal who has fallen beneath them. Ignorance of the Law is no excuse. Helplessness is no excuse. There is no appeal to any Court of error; but prompt execution follows judgment. The innocent child, who ignorantly touches fire, is not the less burned. The man who, in the night, ignorantly walks over a precipice, is not the less destroyed. In nature, therefore, we find no word of pardon for those who have broken the Law, whatever may be their excuse or sorrow. Nor do the intuitions of the soul have much to say of pardon. Conscience, that higher voice of God within us, punishes our errors, rewards our virtues, but says nothing of forgiven sin. In Christ alone do we find a full manifestation of this divine attribute. Christ comes as the representative of God to the fallen, the outcast, the sinful, to show them God's forgiving Love. This forgiving, reconciling Love is the one essential object of Christian faith. And the saving faith of Christianity is a reliance on God's forgiving Love.

§ 33. Christian Faith as the Condition of Forgiveness

The faith, therefore, which is the one condition of forgiveness, is *an act of reliance on the reconciling love of God, shown to us in Christ*. It is essentially, therefore, an ACT, not a belief nor a feeling. So far, indeed, as it is a sight of God's love, it has an intellectual character. So far, too, as it is a loving reliance on that love, it has an affectionate character. But it is in its essence a moral act, an act of choice and will; and yet a receptive act; the opening of the heart to God. It is choosing to lean on him, to repose on his goodness, to rest in the bosom of the Father, to wait on the Lord, and so renew strength. It is ceasing from our own works, that God may work in us and by us. It is "feeding the mind with a wise passiveness," and becoming the channels through which the spirit of God may flow. When we can thus

THE CONDITIONS OF FORGIVENESS.

come near to God, looking away from ourselves, and looking to him with a perfect childlike trust, we may lay down our sins before him, and receive a peace which passes understanding into our soul. This peace is the result of no effort of ours: it is the pure gift of God. All that we have to do is to believe in it, wait for it, and receive it. Faith, then, becomes the organ by which the holy spirit enters the soul, and helps us to cry, Father.

§ 34. Works, growing out of Faith, the Condition of full Salvation.

But what is the place of WORKS, according to this view? If the only condition of forgiveness is Faith, what becomes of Works? The answer follows from what we have before said. Sin, we have seen, has two results: the first, which is estrangement from God, is removed *at once*, when we have faith in his pardoning love. The second, which is moral depravity, is *gradually* removed by faithful continuance in well-doing. We are justified by faith; we are saved by works, flowing out of that reconciled state of the heart. The man who is forgiven is not yet saved. He has the principle of salvation within him, but he must work it out. By the strength which comes to him from union with God, he must build up his character, overcome evil habits, purify his soul from all unworthy desires, and acquire the power of self-denial, generosity, patience, and fidelity, which shall make him a perfect man in Christ Jesus. This is a great work, enough to task all the energy of his soul, and which will develop energies of which he is unconscious. But it is a work which is done, not that he may be pardoned, but because he has been pardoned; not as taskwork done by a servant for wages, but the free and glad efforts which a friend makes for the sake of a friend. It is not anxious drudgery, done only because it is necessary for something else, but toil which is lightened by the sense of the Divine aid and the Divine love, which strengthens us to perform it, and which brings with it its own immediate reward. The Epistles of Paul are filled with exhortations to good works; but the peculiarity of these exhortations is in the motive appealed to. This motive appealed to is not a selfish one. It is not the fear of Hell, or the hope of Heaven. But Christians are called on, by their sense of gratitude for what has been done for them, because they have been forgiven, because they have been bought with a price, because God has chosen them before the foundation of the world, and has blessed them with infinite blessings in Jesus Christ, to be faithful and to abound in the work of the Lord, knowing that their labor is not in vain.

§ 85 Mutual relation of Faith and Works in the Christian Life.

But, if works proceed from faith, faith also proceeds from works, and each needs the other in order to complete it. Faith gives us energy, and enables us to work successfully. But, while we are working, we feel the need of greater faith, and are led to seek for it and obtain it. The two, therefore, become inseparably associated in the Christian life; and neither can exist or thrive without the other. We see a work to be done, a duty to be performed; and, conscious of our inability to do it as we ought, we are led to exercise faith in God, to trust ourselves to his help, and to do it in his strength. Thus the sense of duty, the feeling of responsibility, has led to the sense of dependence, has produced an act of faith; but this again immediately impels to action. Through faith in God we become strong, and the performance of duty is no more a task, but a pleasure; and thus faith leads to works, and works to faith; and no one can say which is the first, and which the second. In the logical order, faith precedes works; but, in the chronological order, they are simultaneous.

§ 86. *Results of Forgiveness in the Future Life.*

But what is the final result of forgiveness hereafter? This is the question we must next proceed to consider. And first we say, that each forgiven soul, being reconciled to God, and at one with him, and feeling itself his child, must be filled with God's love and joy, to its utmost capacity. Evil may still adhere to it; it may not yet have got rid of the consequences of wrong-doing: but this evil is only negative evil, it is only the absence of good. It is incompleteness, smaller capacity, less power; a less degree of faith, hope, and love. Forgiveness has removed the antagonism of the soul to God; and in this antagonism, this wilful perversion, this determined hostility to goodness, consists the whole positive character of sin. All this wilful perversity is changed into willing submission and loving obedience, by the forgiving act of God. The evil that remains, therefore, must be purely negative. But this negative evil, this absence of good, will have its effect on the position of the soul in God's universe. The reason of things and the tenor of the New Testament equally lead to the opinion, that, in the other life, as in this, there will be an ascending scale of being, a gradation, and an order. While all forgiven souls are equal in one respect, their position in another respect will be different. Equal in their inward sense of God's loving nearness, they will be different in their outward faculties and powers, and in the service which they are able to render, — the work they are able to do. Possessing different degrees of insight, energy, and love, some will preside over ten cities, some over five, and others over two. Thus may be reconciled the doctrine of Retribution, taught in the parable of the ten pounds (Luke, xix. 12), with the parable of the laborers in the vineyard (Matt. xx.); the first of which teaches that each is rewarded in proportion to his effort, while the other teaches that the man who had wrought but one hour is made equal with those who have wrought the whole day. Outwardly, in his relation to others and to the universe, each one is placed according to his fidelity; while inwardly, in their rela-

THE CONDITIONS OF FORGIVENESS.

tion to God, all forgiven souls are equal. Thus can be reconciled Mercy and Justice, Law and Love. Thus will the Sacred Order of the universe be maintained; but all parts brought into a perfect harmony, the highest and the lowest being in fulness of sympathy and entire accordance. So will Mercy and Truth meet together, Righteousness and Peace kiss each other.

§ 37. Objections to this Doctrine, and the Answer to them.

Let us now proceed to consider some of the objections which may be urged against this doctrine. The doctrine of forgiveness immediate and entire, on the simple condition of faith, is unfavorable (it may be said) to moral effort. If we can be pardoned freely, on the condition of faith without works, it is argued that we shall not be likely to work. A similar objection appears to be taken notice of by Paul. "Some might say, Let us continue in sin, that grace may abound." He replies, " But how can those who are dead to sin live any longer therein?" His answer amounts to this, that forgiveness produces a dislike to sin, and a wish to do right; that those who are forgiven, love right-doing, and therefore there is no danger of their omitting to work. A new and stronger motive for moral effort is substituted in place of that which is taken away. All experience confirms this, and shows that there are none so active in the service of God, in the performance of duty, in working for human advancement, as those who feel that God has freely forgiven them by his grace. The love and joy thus created in the heart is a perpetual spring of action. So far, therefore, as he who is forgiven is concerned, so far as regards the penitent, this seems a sufficient answer to the objection. But more than this. If this motive of love be not enough to produce moral effort, we must remember that there is still a retribution to which he must look forward, — strict and inevitable. His power of serving God hereafter will depend upon his fidelity here. And the prospect of this inevitable retribution, which no forgiveness can annul, while it animates the Christian to new effort, alarms the impenitent, and leads him to turn to God. Another objection, the opposite to this, may be urged by those who are discouraged because forgiveness does not remove *all* the consequences of sin. They think it discouraging that the forgiven sinner should be obliged to submit to the Law of Retribution, and endure any penalty on account of his past sin. The objection is, that forgiveness is not full and perfect, unless it immediately removes all the consequences of wrong-doing. But to this we may answer, first, that the New Testament itself, in the Parable of the Ten Pounds, plainly teaches that those who are saved come nevertheless under a strict law of Retribution, and are rewarded in different degrees, according to their past fidelity. This doctrine, which is found throughout the New Testament, must not be explained away or omitted, as it usually has been, in

any theory of the future life. And, in the
second place, we may say that he who is
forgiven in the sense which we have described
must be satisfied with his outward lot, wherever
it may be. The forgiveness which unites the
soul with God, and which fills it with the
love of God, is enough. He will gladly take
his place in the great order of the universe,
whatever that place may be, and do honor to
the holy law of God by a glad submission
to its requirements. He will be glad to do
his Master's work in a lowly place and a
lowly office, if it is right that he should be
there. He will rejoice that others stand higher
than himself among the thrones, principalities,
and powers of the heavenly world, since it is
the decree of divine wisdom that it should
be so. It is only our earthly selfishness, not
our Christian feeling, which can complain of
God's forgiveness as imperfect, because it
only gives us the full love of God, and does
not raise us as high as his more faithful
servants. The Prodigal Son, in the Parable,

may teach such objectors a lesson of humility. Neither of these objections to our view of Forgiveness seems to be important, and we may therefore pass on to more serious difficulties.

PART IV.

OBSTACLES AND HELPS.

§ 38. Practical Difficulty of believing in Forgiveness, arising from the Conscience.

THE objections urged against this view of forgiveness from the side of the intellect are easily answered. But the practical difficulty of believing in forgiveness is much greater than the intellectual. It is much easier to believe that the sins of David were forgiven, or the sins of Peter were forgiven, than to believe that our own sins can be forgiven. But what we have to do is not to believe in the forgiveness of David or of Peter, but in our own. And the difficulty arises, not from fear, but from conscience. It is the conscience which makes it difficult to believe in forgiveness. We think we have *no right to be forgiven.* For conscience in every man decides all questions according to the moral standard, and the views of right and wrong, to which each man has attained. Now, the moral standard of one who is not a Christian leads him to believe it his duty not to forgive, but to punish. He has not learned to forgive others, and he cannot therefore believe that he himself may be forgiven. He thinks that society would be injured, if severe punishments were abolished; and he is obliged, by the law of his own mind, to believe that the government of God would be shaken, if God should forgive instead of punishing. Educated by the opinion around us and by our own treatment of others to disbelieve in the power of mercy, and to rely on force and fear, the necessary result is that we cannot believe it possible for God to forgive freely without punishing. In this way, therefore, the assertion of Christ is strictly verified, that, if we forgive not others their trespasses, neither will God forgive us our trespasses. He will not forgive us till we have faith in his forgiving love; for that is the condition of forgiveness. And we cannot believe in his forgiving love, so long as we do not ourselves practise forgiveness; for conscience compels us to judge all cases by the same law. And thus it is that all of our sinfulness, selfishness, and hardness of heart, which leads us first to do wrong, and then to excuse our wrong-doing, sophisticates and perverts the moral sense, and then re-acts upon ourselves. When we have succeeded in persuading ourselves that we ought to be vindictive and unforgiving to others, we persuade ourselves, at the same time, that God ought to be vindictive and unforgiving toward ourselves. For, "to the merciful man, God will show himself merciful, and to the pure he will show himself pure." But to the unmerciful he will necessarily appear unmerciful. Here, then, we see a practical difficulty, which prevents our believing in forgiveness,—a difficulty

OBSTACLES AND HELPS. 93

which remains after all intellectual objections are answered.

§ 39. All Moral Training makes it more difficult.

But not only does all sin increase the difficulty of believing in forgiveness, but all our moral training increases the difficulty also. All moral training quickens the conscience, makes it sensitive, and leads us to look in the direction of law, rather than in that of love. A habit of mind is formed which leads us to contemplate every thing in its relation to the moral law. We look at Retribution until it becomes difficult to believe in pardon. It is not that moral culture lays too much stress on the doctrine of Retribution, but, by laying exclusive stress on that doctrine, it becomes difficult to realize the antagonist doctrine.

§ 40 Christ's Revelation of Divine Love alone makes it possible.

Here, then, we see the difficulties which were to be surmounted by means of the gospel of Christ. In the first place, sin estranges the soul from God; and, when estranged from God, the moral power which should conquer sin is palsied. Then conscience itself increases the evil, by leading us to believe that we have no right to come to God; that we are not worthy to speak to him, or feel toward him the confidence and affection of a child. All our own implacable and unforgiving actions and feelings increase the difficulty, by leading us to attribute the like disposition to the Almighty. The light of Nature cannot help us; for Nature teaches, not pardon, but Law. The intuitions of the soul cannot help us; for they say nothing of forgiveness; moral culture does not help us, but rather increases the difficulty by giving a disproportionate importance in our minds to the doctrine of Retribution. Yet it is evident, that only by being brought into union with God can any new life or spiritual power be obtained. We can do nothing to effect this. God himself, therefore, must come to us; for we are morally unable to go to him. This he does in the gospel, — the essential meaning of which is, that God is in Christ, reconciling the world to himself, not imputing their trespasses unto them. This is the substance of the gospel. The gospel is a new and peculiar manifestation which God makes to men in Jesus Christ. This manifestation is love; as it is written, " God so LOVED the world that he gave his only-begotten Son, that whoso believeth on him should not perish, but have eternal life." And this leads us to ask, What are the agencies which co-operate in human forgiveness? And we shall find, that, for the forgiveness of every human being, something has been done; *first* by God, *next* by Christ, *thirdly* by the Church, and *lastly* by the sinner himself.

§ 41. The Work of God in Human Forgiveness.

What is the work of God in human forgiveness? It is to make *a new and special revelation of himself* to man. As the sinner has made himself incapable of returning to

God, God turns to him. Christianity shows that the Divine Being is also a personal being; not a mere collection of laws; something more than the order of the universe. In him are united both Law and Love; an immutable moral nature, which is the basis of all moral distinction, and a perfectly free will, not bound by the laws of this nature, but perpetually originating new movements. If Christianity be true, that view is false which makes the Deity nothing else than the support of already existing laws. This view widely diffused, and more often believed than expressed, really makes the Deity less free than man himself. For man moves in the twofold sphere of moral character and moral freedom. A wise and good parent, in his intercourse with his children, adopts and maintains certain laws or rules of action, but does something more than this. There is, beside this, a spontaneous movement of affection and of thought, by which he meets and answers every change in the condition of his children, every new want and desire. The gospel affirms the same thing of the Deity. He also moves in the two spheres of Law and Love, of Nature and Freedom; makes new manifestations of himself, corresponding to the new wants of his creatures; comes to them when they cannot come to him; takes the initiative; not merely answers their prayers, but incites them to pray; not merely rewards their efforts, but supplies new motives to lead to effort. Thus, while in one sphere the Deity appears as the moral order of Creation, He moves in the other sphere as the eternal Father and Friend. The miraculous character of the New Testament history consists essentially in this. The great miracle, underlying all the rest, is the new manifestation of God's character which is made in Christ. But this manifestation was not a single act, beginning and ending with the life of Jesus, but is a constant, continued manifestation made in every age to the believing soul. It is a perpetual miracle, by which God reveals himself in Christ, forgiving sin, and bringing his child back to himself. *The work of God in forgiveness, therefore,* IS A POSITIVE, REAL COMMUNICATION OF HIMSELF THROUGH CHRIST TO THE HUMAN SOUL.

§ 42   The Work of Christ in Human Forgiveness, as a Teacher

We ask, in the second place, *What has Christ done for our forgiveness?* His work, in this respect, was done by his teaching, by his life, and by his death. His teaching unfolds an entirely new view of the Divine Being. This view he makes intelligible in the only way by which it can be made intelligible, — by means of the analogy of the earthly parent. In the earthly parent we see that the most perfect purity and the strictest sense of virtue may be joined with tender compassion for an erring child, and untiring efforts for his reformation. We see the good parent devoting time, thought, means, effort, to bring back to a sense of duty, or to save from utter destruction, the reckless, ungrateful, and abandoned son. Here is something more than strict justice, — something more than the moral law. In the story of the Prodigal Son, Jesus carries to the utmost extent this trait of fatherly character. He says there is MORE JOY IN HEAVEN OVER ONE SINNER THAT REPENTETH, THAN OVER NINETY AND NINE JUST PERSONS THAT NEED NO REPENTANCE. Does God, then, love the sinner better than the saint? Does he feel more interest in the one returning from his wickedness, than in the ninety and nine persisting in their goodness? The answer is, he feels, *not more*, but differently. There is more joy, but not more of love. Yet there is a different kind of love. God, who loves the good with the love of approbation and sympathy, loves the evil with the love of pity and compassion. The love of approbation is greatest for the good; the love of pity, the greatest for the evil. The love of sympathy and approbation increases in proportion to nearness; the love of pity, in proportion to distance. Those who, by patient

continuance in well-doing, have worked out
their own salvation, have freed themselves
almost entirely from selfishness, have become
the children of God, are able to enter into his
thought, able to appreciate his creative energy
and his holy will. But those who have re-
ceded, by their wilful obstinacy and perverse-
ness, to the greatest distance from him, plun-
ging into the blackest night and the coldest
moral death, receive the most of that pitying
love which aims at their rescue and pardon.
And as the joint action of the centripetal and
centrifugal forces maintain the balance of the
physical universe, so is the moral creation of
God bound together and maintained by the
combined action of these two principles.
The teaching of Jesus on this subject, which
is wholly original and unprecedented, presents
a view of God in his Fatherly character absolutely essential to human forgiveness. Jesus,
therefore, can say with strict historic truth,
" No man comes to the Father but by Me;"
for this peculiar revelation of God's love to

OBSTACLES AND HELPS. 101

his erring child belongs to the teaching of Jesus alone. He gives a view of God which neither prophet, lawgiver, nor sage ever dared to imagine, — yet no dead speculation, but a flood of Light which is also warm with Life; and this living Light has illuminated the world.

§ 43. And in his Life

Again, Jesus taught BY HIS LIFE the forgiving love of his Father, and thus became himself the image and manifestation of his Father, — God manifest in the flesh. That principle of mercy, that love of pity, which is the principle in the Divine Being which makes human forgiveness possible, was the great active principle which animated the life of Jesus. He came to seek and to save the lost; and not to call the righteous, but sinners, to repentance. His mercies were pronounced on those who felt themselves poor, empty, naked, and blind. His invitation was to those who were weary and heavy laden. His intercourse was with the publican and sinner.

And wherever he went, he found the penitent to whom he could say, " Thy sins are forgiven thee: go in peace." Those who hated him, and sought to kill him, were the objects of his especial interest. And his last words were those of forgiveness for his ignorant tormentors. Thus the whole spirit of his life was a manifestation of the principle of Forgiving love. We see that there is such a thing by his example; we see it, not as a theory, but realized in action. We are thus enabled to have faith in it. And when we come to know, that this principle, shown in the life of Jesus, is the same principle in God, we are able to have faith in God's forgiving love. Thus Christ's Life, in its totality, helps us to behold and rejoice in this Divine Love, as an actual spiritual reality; helps us to take hold of it by Faith, and feed on it in the heart with thanksgiving.

§ 44 And by his Death. Principal Texts.

We now approach a more difficult question, — difficult on many accounts, but especially because it has been the theme of so much controversy. It is difficult to look at any question which has been the subject of continued controversy, except from the point of view of the disputants of either side. We allow no text to make its natural impression on our mind, but only inquire, as regards each, how it bears upon the old dispute. So far as possible, we will endeavor to avoid this narrowness, while inquiring how the death of Jesus bears upon the Forgiveness of sin. Many passages in the New Testament indicate a connection between these two. First, we have the words of Jesus in instituting the Lord's supper, — "This is my blood of the New Covenant, which is shed for many for the remission of sins" (Matt. xxvi. 28). Next to this come several passages in the Epistles of Paul, and especially the famous passage (Rom. iii. 25), where he says that "God has set forth Jesus to be a propitiation or mercy-seat, through faith in his blood, to declare, or manifest, his mode of forgiving past and present sins." There are other passages which teach that Jesus was "delivered for our offences," or on account of them; that he "died for the ungodly," and that he "died for us while we were yet sinners," and that, "being now justified by his blood, we shall be saved from wrath through him." " For if," continues the apostle (Rom. v. 10), "when we were enemies, we *were reconciled* to God by the DEATH of his Son; much more, being reconciled, we *shall be saved* by his LIFE." These are the principal passages bearing on the subject in the Epistle to the Romans, and are of the first importance as regards the present question. In the two Epistles to the Corinthians, Christ is called "our passover," — is said to have "died for our sins," and that "he died for all;" but no connection is indicated between his death and our forgiveness. In the Epistle to the Ephesians we find many more passages indicating this connection. We have " Redemption through his blood, even forgiveness of sin " (Eph. i. 7).

"But now in Christ Jesus, ye, who sometime were far off, are made nigh by the blood of Christ. For he is our peace, who hath made both Jew and Gentile one, that he might reconcile both unto God in one body by the cross" (Eph. ii. 13, 16). In Eph. iv. 32, we read, "Forgive one another, even as God in Christ hath forgiven you." Similar passages are found in Col. i. 20, ii. 13; 1 Tim. ii. 6; Tit. ii. 14, iii. 4. The Epistle to the Hebrews teaches that Christ made "a sacrifice of himself for sins," and to "bear the sins of many;" and that, "his blood may purge our conscience from dead works." The last passage, indeed, seems to imply a moral influence in the death of Jesus to reform the character, as do other passages like these: — (1 Peter, ii. 24) "Who his own self bore our sins in his own body on the tree, *that we, being dead to sins, should live unto righteousness; by whose stripes ye were healed.*" (1 John, i. 7) "The blood of Jesus Christ *cleanses* us from all sin." (Rev. i. 5) "Who has *washed* us from our sins in his blood." (Titus, ii. 14) "Who gave himself for us, that he might *redeem us from all iniquity*, and PURIFY unto himself a peculiar people, *zealous of good works.*" From all these passages, we see plainly that the doctrine of the New Testament is, that the death of Christ has an intimate connection with the forgiveness of sin. But it is equally plain, that these passages do not clearly teach what this connection is. They assert that the death of Christ is a means of our forgiveness; but they do not at all teach *how* it is the means.

§ 45. Various Theories concerning the Effect of Christ's Death.

The nearest approach to a theory on this subject in the New Testament is to be found in the Epistle to the Hebrews. The writer asserts that the Death of Christ was necessary to the perfection of his character, and that this perfection of Christ's character was necessary for our salvation. But this theory is merely indicated, not elaborated. The next theory which attempted to explain the way in which the death of Christ procured our forgiveness was that of the early Church. The Greek and Latin fathers, during many centuries, taught that the death of Christ was a ransom paid to the Devil to redeem from his power the souls which had legally fallen into his hands, and become his property in consequence of their sins. The next theory was that of Anselm, who taught that the death of Christ was an equivalent for the debt due to God on account of human transgression; and that, the debt being paid, the debtors might be forgiven. This view also prevailed for many hundred years. The next theory was that of Grotius, who taught that the death of Christ was a manifestation of God's displeasure against sin, and was necessary to enable God, as a moral governor, to forgive the sinner, without impairing the respect due to the moral law. This opinion is held more extensively than any other among the Orthodox of the present time. A fourth theory, which has prevailed more extensively among a certain school of Unitarians, is, that the death of Christ is a moral influence exerted upon men to produce repentance and reformation by the power of its example of generous self-sacrifice. For as, according to the view of this school, the only forgiveness possible is that which follows reformation, the death of Christ can only procure our forgiveness by producing reformation.

§ 46. All Matters of Theology not of Religion.

It is not our purpose at this time to enter into a critical examination of these theories; against all of which, however, grave objections seem to lie. We will proceed positively, rather than negatively, by examining anew, and as if for the first time, this question, without further reference to previous theories on the subject. The New Testament declares, as we have seen, that we are forgiven by means of the death of Christ. It applies to his death many of the sacrificial figures of the Jewish ritual, making him sometimes the sin-offering of the new covenant, sometimes the covenant-victim of the new covenant, and again the Christian Paschal Lamb. But as the New Testament says nothing, beyond the use of these various and conflicting images, to point out how it was that the death of Jesus removed the difficulties in the way of human forgiveness, we may safely conclude, that all speculations on this subject are not matters of faith, but only matters of belief and opinion; that they belong to the domain of Theology, not to that of Religion. And, secondly, we may be sure that the most correct theory on this subject must come after each school of thought shall have contributed its own solution of the problem. We therefore proceed to our own explanation.

§ 47. How the Death of Christ may produce Faith in Forgiving Love

The death of Christ must procure forgiveness of sin by removing the difficulties in the way of that forgiveness. In the course of thought we have pursued, we have seen that these difficulties were twofold, arising from the nature of man and from the nature of God. The *subjective difficulty*, or that arising from the nature of man, is the difficulty of believing in the forgiving love of God, because man's conscience shows him that a holy being must necessarily be estranged from an unholy being; and that, in the nature of things, there is a great gulf fixed between righteousness and iniquity. The *objective difficulty*, or that arising from the nature of God, is that this law really exists, and that God really is and must be alienated from every unholy being. These are the two difficulties in the way of human forgiveness, one or both of which must have been removed by the death of Christ. Taking first the subjective difficulty, we see how that may be, in a great measure, removed by the teaching and life of Jesus, both of which we have seen to be a manifestation of the forgiving love of God. We can believe a thing when we see it, the reasons of which we cannot understand. We may not understand how God can forgive us until we are perfectly holy; and yet, if we actually see his forgiving love manifested in the words and life of Jesus, we may be enabled to believe in it. But still more is this manifested in the death of Jesus. When this death is regarded as part of the plan of Divine Providence for the forgiveness and redemption of the sinner, we say, "He who spared not his own Son, but freely gave him up for us all, how shall he not with him freely give us all things?" "If, while we were sinners, Christ died for us," it proves, more than any thing else can, the love which God has even for sinners. If he permits the good, whom he loves as belonging to himself, to suffer for the sinners who are estranged from him, it shows that they also are in some way dear to him. If he not only permits, but decrees, that Jesus, his wellbeloved Son, a being of perfect holiness and purity, therefore perfectly united with himself, shall suffer and die in his work of saving sinners, it proves conclusively the yearning of His soul for their redemption.

§ 48. As, in fact, it has actually done

That, as a matter of fact, the death of Jesus has been the highest manifestation to the world of God's forgiving love, all history proves. Here also the theory is one thing, and may be questioned: the fact is quite another, and is unquestionable. The story of the death of Jesus has touched the human heart, and awakened a faith in the fatherly goodness of God; has produced penitence for sin; has awakened hopes of pardon and salvation, and been the beginning of a new life to tens of thousands. Jesus, being lifted up, has drawn all men unto him. That his death has been a great means of reconciling sinners to God, and removing the subjective difficulty on the side of man, in the way of redemption, no one acquainted with the facts of history will deny.

OBSTACLES AND HELPS. 113

§ 49. How Christ's Death may have satisfied the Divine Holiness.

But what did the death of Jesus do to remove the *Objective difficulty*, or that on the side of the Deity? His death reconciled man to God: did it also reconcile God to man? The scriptures do not positively assert this; but they indicate it in one or two passages. The difficulties connected with this question are greater than most others, and fortunately their solution is not so necessary to our peace of mind as has commonly been supposed. Since God has positively taught and shown us that he is ready to forgive our sins, if we will have faith to believe it, we may be satisfied with this assurance, and not insist upon understanding exactly how it can be done. Here, as elsewhere, we must walk by faith, and not sight. No greater error has ever been committed by Theologians, than when they have made their own theories of the atonement, instead of God himself, the object of faith. God's manifestation of himself in

Christ, as a forgiving God, is the only true object of faith; and any theory which explains the method of this forgiveness can be only an object of belief.* The New Testament itself gives us no theory, but at best only hints and intimations upon which one may be founded. The difficulty on the side of God, lying in the way of human forgiveness, has commonly been supposed to proceed from his attribute of Justice. But the Justice of God is but the Holiness of God manifesting itself in action; and the real and only difficulty (as we have before seen) on the side of the Deity, respecting human forgiveness, arises from the essential repugnance between a holy being and those who are unholy. Forgiveness implies the union of the soul with God. It implies a partaking of the Divine nature. It implies God dwelling in us and we in God, or the most perfect union which language is capable of expressing. But the most sincerely penitent have yet much of impurity connected with their character. How, then, can they be forgiven in any such sense as this? None of the Orthodox theories of the atonement have met this difficulty. They have said that Christ has suffered the penalty due to our sins. But a criminal who has endured the penalty of his crime is not necessarily made holy thereby. If we had endured the penalty ourselves due to our sins, this would not have made us holy. Supposing that Christ has endured the penalty due to human sin, all that logically follows from this is, that men are released thereby from suffering this penalty themselves. They escape from Hell; but escape from Hell is no preparation for Heaven. Therefore a deeper difficulty remains, which this theory cannot remove. Aware of this, the older and more logical Orthodox theologians added a second part to their theory of the atoning work of Christ. By his passive obedience, they said, he paid the penalty due to our sins; and his active obedience, or holiness, was transferred or imputed to us, and becomes ours. We become holy by means of the righteousness of Christ which is imputed to us. But, beside other difficulties which lie against this scheme, there is this, which is a fatal one, that what we need is not imputed righteousness, but real righteousness. The difficulty in the way of our forgiveness is not a technical one, but a real one. It does not come from any outward law, but from the holy nature of the Deity himself. We are, then, irresistibly brought to this conclusion,— that, if there be any objective difficulty in the way of human forgiveness, it must be from the essential hostility of the Holy character of God to all unholiness. And again, that, if Christ's death removes this difficulty, it must be by communicating to the sinner his own perfect holiness, — by removing from his soul the essential nature of sin, and by making him really, not legally, holy in the sight of God.

§ 50. By communicating Actual Holiness.

It is with a feeling of awe and adoring reverence that we are brought to this great conclusion, — a conclusion justified by the language of the New Testament throughout. Shall we believe then, that, *when we are born of God, we do not and cannot commit sin, for that his seed remains in us; and that we cannot sin because we are born of God?* Is it true that Christ's death was necessary to his own perfection, so "*that, being perfect, he might become the author of eternal salvation to those who obey him*"? Is it true that faith in Christ so unites us with him, that the germ of his perfect righteousness is planted within our souls, not being merely imputed, but actually *imparted*, to us? So the scriptures plainly teach, asserting that the new life within us is the life of Christ as to its principle; and that the life we live, we live by faith in the Son of God. They teach that we become dead to sin, and alive to righteousness; and that, being sometime alienated and enemies in our mind by wicked works, we have been reconciled by the death of Christ, that we might be presented holy, blameless, and without fault, before the eye of God (Col. i. 22). The evil which remains connected with the soul is no more part of it. It is external to it. The centre of the soul is LOVE, which is pure and perfect. Christ dwells in the heart by faith, and the root and ground of the soul is Love (Eph. iii. 17). The soul, inwardly renewed, is toward God created anew in righteousness and pure holiness (Eph. iv. 24). Sin, therefore, has no more dominion over us. It is not our master; for we do not submit to it nor love it. It may sometime overpower us; but we are not its slave. For morally we are only the servants of that to which we yield ourselves to obey. The mind serves the law of God; and if, through weakness or error, we do any evil, it is not we that do it, but the evil habit external to the soul which has not yet been wholly cast off by the power of the new principle.

We are not in the flesh, but in the spirit; for
the spirit of God dwells in us. And if Christ
be in us, the body indeed may still have some
of the death of sin adhering to it; but the
spirit is filled with the life of righteousness
(Rom. viii. 10). That is to say, that, when a
man is able to believe in God's forgiving love
through Christ, the inmost principle of his
nature, being united with Christ, becomes
wholly pure, and all unholiness is rooted out
of it. Any evil that remains is external
to the soul, and belongs to the body. But
that, too, shall be purified and cast out by the
operation of this new principle. Even, as
the apostle goes on to say (Rom. viii. 11),
that, if the Divine Spirit dwell within us, it
will make alive our bodies also, and make
them spiritual too. This doctrine, however
will not encourage presumption, or enable us
to continue contented in sin; for the only
evidence which we can have of being thus
inwardly pure is that we abhor all evil,
and, by the help of the spirit, do mortify

(or kill out) the deeds of the body. While we are loving God and holiness, and only so long, are we inwardly free from the power of sin.

§ 51. *The Work of Man in his own Forgiveness.*

Having considered the work of God and of Christ, we now ask what man himself has to do in order to be forgiven. The condition on his part, as we have seen, is faith alone. But we have also seen, that this faith is by no means a barren intellectual principle, but an active reliance on the Divine mercy; and that it implies, as its own necessary condition, certain antecedents. It implies *a sense of sin;* for, unless we perceive the reality of sin, we can by no means perceive the reality of pardon. It is plainly impossible for one who is not conscious of his sinfulness to feel the deep meaning of forgiveness. In some form or other, therefore, the feeling of alienation must precede that of reconciliation. The sense of estrangement and opposition must go before that of union. Those who, with the deepest humility, are most profoundly sensible of their own moral weakness, who are most crushed by the sense of unworthiness, whose conscience is most painfully alive to every omission of duty, — are prepared, so far, for the most exulting happiness, the most rejoicing faith in Divine mercy. Where sin abounds, there grace may much more abound. But this sense of sin is awakened by the Law; and the more high and pure the law, the more thorough is the work of preparation which it accomplishes. Hence, in the nature of things, the Law must precede the Gospel with every individual, as in the order of history, the Mosaic law prepared the Jewish nation for the coming of Christ. But, since the coming of Christ, the Gospel itself performs also the work of the Law. Christianity sets before men the highest standard of duty; gives them a moral ideal so lofty, pure, and spiritual, that nothing can more thoroughly reveal the difference between what they ought to be, and what they are. By exciting to moral effort, it makes clear to us this difference. Thus the Gospel, the chief work of which is to make man one with God, has a subordinate and preparatory work to do in showing him his separation from God. For not till the contradiction is clearly revealed can the agreement be effected. Not till the antithesis is brought out can the synthesis be accomplished.

§ 52   His Efforts to do Right prepare him for Forgiveness.

We see, therefore, that faith in God's forgiving love, which is the one condition of forgiveness, is nevertheless itself conditioned by the sense of sin. But this sense of sin has also its own condition, which is the desire and the effort to attain goodness. Nothing but a sincere desire and earnest effort to be and do right will produce a real conviction of our deficiencies. Any conviction of sin, not based on this, must be transient, because superficial. The conscience may be momentarily roused by descriptions of an offended God and an impending doom. But when thus awakened, unless a genuine desire for goodness on its own account succeed, the sense of sin will prove itself a shallow impression, not a permanent conviction. But every sincere wish and prayer for goodness, every earnest attempt to fulfil difficult duty, is sure to help on our spiritual progress, either directly or indirectly. By one road or another, every such effort brings us nearer to God. If the effort to do right succeeds, it goes to form a righteous habit of mind, increases our moral purity, and so brings us nearer to God by the direct road of moral likeness to him. If the effort fails, it shows us our own weakness, marks the amount of separation between the soul and God, produces a conviction of sin, and so prepares for our union with God by the indirect road of faith and forgiveness. Hence it is that purity of heart is made the blessed condition of the sight of God. Hence the hunger and thirst after righteousness is blessed with the promise of satisfaction. Faith, therefore, is the only condition of forgiveness; but it implies a true humility, and a sincere desire for goodness.

§ 53. Repentance. its relation to Faith.

It will be asked, Is not REPENTANCE also a condition of Forgiveness? Unquestionably it is; but it need not be mentioned separately, since our description of faith includes it. Repentance is simply turning from sin to God. But he who comes to God in trusting reliance, humbly conscious of his sin, earnestly desiring goodness, has evidently, in this act of faith, also performed the act of repentance. Repentance and faith thus appear to be the two sides of the same act of the soul in turning to God. Considered in relation to sin, it is repentance. Considered in relation to God and the good, it is faith. Like the magnet, the soul is repelled on the one side and attracted on the other at the same moment;

repelled from evil, and attracted by goodness. But it is one and the same polar force which acts in both directions, and we may describe it either by the name of repentance, or by the name of faith.

§ 54. Is Faith Man's Work or God's Gift?

But we have now reached a difficult point of inquiry. This act of faith — is it the work of man, or the work of God? Is it in our power to have faith, if we will? or must God help us to it by a divine influence? The scriptures command us to have faith. Jesus says, "*Have faith in God;*" condemns its absence, rewards its presence. On the other hand, Paul says expressly, that it is "by grace" we "are saved through faith, and *that not of ourselves, but it is the gift of God.*" Yet Paul himself commanded the jailer at Philippi to "believe on the Lord Jesus Christ." And, in our experience, faith, when we exercise it, seems to be our own act; and yet it often seems to be more difficult than any thing else. There are times, which all Christians have experienced, in which faith becomes almost an impossibility; in which we can only say, "Help our unbelief;" in which God seems to have withdrawn that love which is the object of faith, so that we can no longer behold it or lean upon it. But, at such times as these, we usually feel that we can only wait on the Lord, wait his time, be not weary of waiting, and cherish and hold fast the little faith that we have, until he shall give us more. Scripture, therefore, and experience both ascribe Faith to man's effort and to God's gift; and both seem necessary to its production.

§ 55. God and Man concur in each Act of Faith.

Christian experience and the New Testament seem, then, to bring us to the conclusion, that faith is an act of the soul in which God and man concur; God manifesting his love, and man relying upon it. The holy spirit, or that inward influence which is rep-

OBSTACLES AND HELPS. 127

resented as coming from God through Christ, to form Christ within us, shows to the heart the forgiving love of God. Our work is to open our heart to receive this influence, thankfully to accept it, firmly to repose upon it. The act of faith, therefore, is a concurrent act of God and man: the objective side, or the object of faith, being a gift of God's spirit; the subjective side, or the reception of this love, being man's work.

§ 56. What Man can do for himself, and where he must stop.

Still the question recurs, What, and how much, can man do? Let us suppose a case in order to make this point clear, and such an one as continually occurs in the intercourse of every Christian minister with the members of his society. A young man or a young woman comes to him, and says, " I wish to be better than I am; I feel that I ought to be; I wish to be a Christian; I have tried to be one; I have endeavored to do my daily duties in a Christian spirit. But I seem to make no progress; I feel as far from God as ever; my heart is cold; I have not the love for God which I wish I had, nor the happiness in my duties which I ought to have." Now, if what we have thus far said be true, a person in this state of mind has the conviction of sin of which we have spoken, and needs the sense of forgiveness. He needs to be reconciled to God by the reception of God's forgiving love. Say this to him, therefore, and convince him of it, — convince him that Christ came to bring pardon to those in just his state of mind, and that in this pardon he will find both the love, the joy, and the strength he needs. Let us suppose him to be convinced of this, and he says, "How shall I obtain this forgiveness?" You answer, "By Faith. That is the whole. Have faith in God's forgiving love." But he answers again, "This is the very difficulty. I have no faith. I cannot exercise it, because I do not possess it. This is just what I want." The minister naturally replies to this, "Then pray for it," and quotes the promises of Christ to show that God will always give his holy spirit to those who ask him. He answers, "But, to pray aright, I must pray in faith; and, when you tell me to pray, you suppose me already to possess that which I am seeking." Now, the minister may properly and justly encourage this inquirer to believe that he has *some* faith at least, if it be only like a grain of mustard-seed, and by means of this he may obtain more. But the minister may do something more than this. He may continue to press upon the inquirer all the passages of Scripture and all the facts which his experience has made him acquainted with, by which to enable this Seeker to believe in God's present forgiving love. He will be to him what Ambrose was to Augustine, what Staupitz was to Luther, what Peter Bohler and the Moravians were to Wesley, — he will be a mediator, by means of the faith which he has himself received, to produce a like faith in the mind of the other. When he can do nothing else, he can kneel down, and pray with him and for him, and thus may be the means of increasing his faith, and enabling him to pray himself.

§ 57. The Work of the Christian Church

Now this account illustrates the work which THE CHRISTIAN CHURCH has to do with forgiveness. The Christian Church may be regarded as *the body of Christ*, by which his spirit still acts upon the earth to create faith in human souls; or it may be regarded as the channel through which that principle of life which entered the world with Christ has continued to flow on from age to age. The Church, in its ideal character, is thus the medium by which Christ communicates himself to the world. And all actual churches are living and true churches, just in proportion as they approximate to this ideal. The Church has a twofold work; first, to the World; and, second, to its own members. In relation to the World, its work is Evan-

OBSTACLES AND HELPS. 131

gelical and Missionary; and its object is to convert it and to humanize it. In relation to its own members, its duty is edification and consolation, — to make them strong and to make them happy. Now, the means by which it accomplishes these objects are not exhausted when we have named Preaching and Teaching, Public Worship, Prayer and Praise, Social meetings, and Meetings for active benevolence. Its chief means and its highest prerogative remain unspoken; for these are both to be found in its own living faith. It is faith which produces faith. There is a text in the New Testament long perverted to the support of outward Church authority and formal ecclesiastical pretensions, which in its true sense shows us wherein consists the essential power and real authority of the Christian Church. We read (Matt. xvi. 13), that Jesus on one occasion asked one of his disciples what was said of him; and when Peter gave as his own testimony this declaration, "Thou art the Christ, the Son of the living God," Jesus answered, "Blessed art thou, Simon Barjonah; for flesh and blood have not revealed this to thee, but my Father who is in Heaven." He had not been taught it by man, but by God. It was not a hearsay opinion, but a personal conviction. It was not a Belief resting on the testimony of others, but a Faith, the object of which was a divine revelation to his soul. So likewise Paul says (Gal. i. 16), " When it pleased God to reveal his Son in me, I conferred not with flesh and blood." Then Jesus, proceeding, declares that upon this rock-like faith in Peter, and in the other apostles, he would build his Church; digging deep through the soil of opinion, and the shifting sand of a hearsay belief, down to a solid, God-inspired faith. Then he adds, " I will give to thee the Keys of the Kingdom of Heaven; and whatsoever thou shalt bind on earth shall be bound in heaven, and whatsoever thou shalt loose on earth shall be loosed in heaven." The promise here made to Peter is repeated (Matt.

xviii. 18) to all the disciples. What, then, is this power? It is the power which faith has of creating faith. It is itself the key to the kingdom of heaven, by which the door may be bound or loosed; that is, opened or shut. In the order of Providence, it depends upon him to whom God has given faith, whether others around him shall have faith or be without it. If he is true to his faith, if his life is rooted in it, if his words are colored by it, if his tone and temper are constantly informed by this pure and subtle spirit, then he carries with him a sphere of influence by which to produce a like faith in all who are prepared to receive it. God to him is no name, but a reality; Christ, not an historical Messiah, but a present Saviour; eternal life, no future, but a present immortality. By the contagion of this faith, he awakens like convictions in other minds; and to them also God in the Soul, Righteousness, Eternity, and Heaven come forth from the region of abstractions into that of realities. This is the true key to the kingdom of Heaven; and, in the famous passage to which we give this interpretation, Jesus is impressing the responsibility which rests upon those who have this key of faith in their possession. So surely as they neglect to use it, the door of heaven remains closed. And those who, by the sight of their faith, might have been quickened into a new life, remain, through their negligence, where they were before. This responsibility and privilege belongs not to Peter alone, nor to the Apostles alone, nor to bishops, priests, and preachers alone, but to every man to whose heart, as to that of Peter, God has made a revelation of the reality of spiritual things. But, with regard to forgiveness of sins, the sphere, duty, and work of the living Church is declared in that other famous passage (John, xx. 22, 23), where we read that Jesus after his resurrection said to his disciples, "As my Father hath sent me, even so send I you;" and then, breathing on them, added, "Receive the Holy Ghost. Whose sins ye remit, they are remitted; and whose sins ye retain, they are retained." It is evident that Jesus could not have intended to give to his disciples the power of deciding arbitrarily whose sins should be forgiven, and whose not. So evident indeed is this, that even the Church of Rome has never ventured to claim for its priesthood any such power. The priestly absolution depends for its efficacy, according to the Roman Catholic doctrine, upon the state of mind of the penitent. If the penitence is not sincere, the absolution goes for nothing.* Accordingly, the power to forgive sins claimed by the Roman priesthood amounts only to this, that they may tell a man who confesses his sins, that, if his penitence is sincere, his sin is forgiven. But the words of Christ seem to imply more than this. They seem to imply, that as Christ

* The sacrament of Penance, according to the Council of Trent (fourteenth Session), has, on the part of the penitent, three essential acts, namely, of Contrition, Confession, and Satisfaction; and, on the part of the Priest, the absolving words, "I absolve thee."

was the medium by whom God has communicated to the world forgiveness; so, too, his disciples are the media through whom Christ communicates forgiveness Now, we see that this is actually the fact, if the condition of forgiveness be faith, and if the faith of one be the means of producing faith in another. This being so, the words of Christ must be understood as teaching the great privilege and responsibility of those who thus become, in the order of Providence, the necessary instruments and agencies for communicating to others the forgiving love of God.

§ 58. The Twofold Work of the Church in Forgiveness.

The work of the Church in the Forgiveness of Sin is twofold. First, by preaching the Law to awaken the desire for goodness, the effort for obedience, and the sense of separation from God; and, secondly, by preaching the Gospel, to produce the knowledge of forgiveness, and to communicate, through its own faith, that faith which will bring pardon. To those who are already seeking for pardon and faith, the Church should feel itself to be the appointed and natural agency by which pardon is to be obtained. When the seeker is unable to have faith for himself, the Church should have faith for him. When he is discouraged, the Church should have courage for him. When he would despair, the Church should hope for him. When he cannot pray for himself, the Church should pray for him. For if the Church has faith in forgiveness and in the power of prayer, it should exercise that faith on behalf of those who are unable to exercise it for themselves. And, in point of fact, this is what all sincere and practical Christians actually endeavor to do. In all churches there are those who, by their words and their prayers, endeavor to bring faith to those who need it; and they thus become in reality the means by which it is obtained. But what is wanted is, that the whole Christian Church should understand that these efforts are its legitimate work, and that it should reverently and joyfully accept the great privilege to which its Master has called it. And also that it should do its work, not occasionally as a doubtful experiment, but in the conviction that it has been made the certain and appointed channel through which faith and forgiveness shall come. When the Christian Church has learned its duties and privileges, it will be able to show to each seeking soul the way of Salvation, and enable him to enter it. It will be able to remove all doubt and all uncertainty as to what each one must do to be saved. As the types and shadows of the Jewish ritual were fulfilled by the realities of the Gospel, so will the Roman Catholic sacrament of confession and absolution be fulfilled by the Church, which has become the medium of communicating, not an external and formal Remission of Sins, but an inward and real Sense of Pardon. For this sacrament, which has come down from the middle ages, will stand as a symbol till it is replaced by the reality, — will remain as a promise till it is removed by the fulfilment of the promise. Men go to the Catholic Church because it seems to offer them a surer outward aid and help. But this help is formal, technical, not living and human. Something greater and better is needed; and something better, as God lives, shall yet come.

PART V.

RESULTS OF FORGIVENESS.

§ 59   The New Life growing out of Forgiven Sin.

WE next pass on to consider the nature of the new life growing out of forgiveness. For Christianity in the soul is, in the strict and literal sense, a NEW LIFE. And by this we mean, not merely a new course of action and conduct, but the formation of a new vital principle. As the temporal life of man or animal consists, not merely in outward actions, but also in an invisible principle by which those actions are prompted; so the spiritual life consists, not merely in new efforts and actions, but in the possession of a new principle, out of which these actions naturally flow. Therefore Christianity, as to its

RESULTS OF FORGIVENESS.   141

inward principle in the soul, is constantly described in the New Testament as a *life*. This eternal life is not merely immortality in the future world, for it is spoken of as a gift specially bestowed *upon Christians* as the consequence of their faith (John, iii. 15, vi. 47); nor is it the future happiness of the good hereafter alone, for it is spoken of as something abiding in the soul *here* (John, vi. 54, 47, v. 24). The analogy of the spiritual life to temporal life appears in many particulars. As temporal life begins with our birth, so the spiritual life begins with the new birth. As the temporal life is supported by food, so the spiritual life has its food also, which is the body and blood of Christ; in other words, his whole human history, his active and passive virtue, his energy to do, and his patience to bear; which must be not merely looked at, thought about, and remembered, but, like the food which we take into the body, become a part of ourselves. As our earthly existence is divided into rest and labor, repose and action, night and day; so the spiritual life consists of alternations of faith and works, trust and obedience, prayer and labor, quiet waiting and active obedience. In our temporal life we are surrounded by Nature; by sky and earth; mountain, forest, and ocean; drifting clouds, falling rains, the vegetable and animal worlds; and the speaking face of man and woman. In our spiritual life we are surrounded by a Spiritual World of holy truths, gentle affections, far-reaching hopes, noble aims, and sympathies wide as the world. As the vital principle of plant or bird shows itself especially in the fact of growth, so one characteristic of the spiritual life is development and progress. The largest definition, perhaps, which can be given of the term life, is DEVELOPMENT. All life is the development, unfolding, growth, of a germ; and life is thus the perpetual unfolding of the hidden principle of each seed, according to its own laws, under certain external influences. These influences are all attractions: the seed of the

RESULTS OF FORGIVENESS. 143

plant is developed by the attractions of light, heat, air, water, earth. The life of the animal is developed by the attractions of food, the joy of muscular motion, and similar pleasures. Man's soul is developed, as regards this life, by the various objects which attract his desires and passions. The law of life, therefore, is development; and development takes place under the influence of those external objects whose attractions awaken the latent appetite. Just so the spiritual life is the development of the spirit by the attractions of eternal things, which awaken love. "All life," says Fichte, "is love. He who loves most, lives most." And love, therefore, in the New Testament, is justly made the essence of the spiritual life. We have, then, this correspondence complete thus far between the temporal and spiritual life. Each has a principle which is to develop and grow. In each this growth is produced by the attraction of external objects, which awakens Desire in the one case, and in the other desire in the higher form of

Love. The organ by which these external objects are perceived, in the one case, is the body with its senses; in the other, that intuition which we have called Faith. If it be said that we have described Faith as an *act* rather than as a *sight*, as reliance on love rather than as the perception of it, — we may reply that the correspondence holds good even here; for we perceive the external world by an *active* sensation, just as we exercise faith in unseen things by an active intuition.

§ 60 The Twofold Character of this Life, and of Goodness generally.

This new Life in the Soul is, in its essence, LOVE; and, by means of its organ Faith, renews itself continually from on High. But this Life in the Soul has a twofold character, and acts in a twofold direction. It alternates between labor and rest, effort and repose, activity and receptivity, obedience to the law and trust in the gospel. *Christian* Goodness, therefore, differs from the Goodness of Nature in being *principle*, and from the Goodness of Morality in being *spontaneous;* and is the purest union and harmony of both kinds. For Goodness in general is of these two kinds, consisting of Intention on the one side, and Character on the other. The Goodness of Morality or Intention consists in effort, struggle, and conflict; and is esteemed great in proportion to the temptation resisted, the trial borne, the obstacle encountered, the difficulty overcome. The Goodness of Nature or Character is not conflict, but harmony; not struggle, but attainment. It consists in natural good tendencies and pure tastes, or in acquired habits of goodness. The Goodness of Intention is meritorious; the Goodness of Attainment is beautiful. We respect the first; we love the second. The absence of one implies guilt; the absence of the other implies depravity. He who does not try to do right and to become good is guilty. He who has no love for goodness, no true, kind, and noble tendencies, is depraved. The seat of the one is the conscience or will; the seat of the other is the instinct or natural tendencies. Now, the will is determined toward goodness through the conscience. We choose goodness because we feel that we ought to do so. The heart is determined toward goodness by its perception of moral duty. We love goodness because it appears to us beautiful. The conscience is commanded; the desires, instincts, tendencies, are attracted. All which *commands* the will through the conscience, we may call the Law; and all which *attracts* the Affections toward goodness by a manifestation of its Beauty, we may call the Gospel.

That this distinction is real, and no mere distinction of words, will appear if we consider how often these two kinds of Goodness are found separate. Many good men have no beauty in their goodness; and many beautiful characters have no strength with their beauty. We esteem the first, but are unable to love them; we are attracted toward the last, but cannot esteem them.

Now, it has been a usual fault, both with moral and religious teachers, first, not to notice and distinguish these two different kinds of goodness; or, secondly, to undervalue the Goodness of Nature and tendency, when compared with that of Resolve and effort. As, in the fable of "The Lion and the Painter," the Lion was always represented as conquered by the man, because the man was always the painter; so here it has happened, that the Moralist has always overestimated the goodness of morality. The Instincts and the Affections do not write moral treatises. The conscious, intelligent, deliberate purpose of Right-doing is more apt to appear in our ethical writings than the spontaneous and unpremeditated goodness which never thinks of composing its own biography. Some Moralists and Theologians even go so far as to make *all* goodness to consist in conscious, deliberate effort and struggle. But not only is this palpably false, but it is also evident that the Goodness of Intention is by no means superior to the Goodness of Tendency. For, if it were, it would follow that a sinner struggling against his sin, struggling against foul habits and depraved appetites, is better than that soul, angel-born and angel-bred, which knows no such struggle, because its tastes are all pure, and its appetites not depraved. Moreover, it would follow that the worst of sinners, provided he was struggling against his sin, is better than the highest saint or angel nearest God's throne, whose soul tends steadily towards truth and goodness;

> "Whose love is an unerring light,
> Whose joy, its own security."

Further still, we must ask what struggle and conflict there can be in the Goodness of God. His Goodness, doubtless, is conscious and deliberate; but he is not tempted with evil, and can have no conflicts with himself. The Goodness of God, toward which good men aim, is not a goodness of conflict and struggle. And, further still, if we say that the goodness of effort is higher than that of tendency, we are brought to the paradoxical conclusion that a man grows worse as he grows better. For, as he grows better, he finds it *easier* to do right, his moral tastes become stronger, his evil appetites weaker, he is attracted more and more toward all things excellent, and consequently there is less of effort, and more of impulse, in his goodness. The probable result, therefore, of these considerations is, that there are these two kinds of goodness, and that they are equally venerable and holy.

§ 61 The Christian Life the Synthesis of both kinds of Goodness.

The essential peculiarity of the Christian Life is, that it is the complete harmony, THE ABSOLUTE SYNTHESIS OF BOTH KINDS OF GOODNESS. It distinguishes them, in order that it may unite them. It is able to unite them, because it has first distinguished them. Christian faith, revealing the high *Law of God*, awakens the conscience, and rouses the will to effort to overcome all evil. Christian faith, revealing the abounding *Love of God*, creates new affections, and attracts the soul upward, ascending by its proper motion. The love of God moves us to effort; the effort enables us more entirely to rely upon and realize His love. Faith and Works; Love and Labor; Prayer and Action; the Reception of the Holy Spirit, and the Endeavor to impart it, — these follow each other like Day and Night; repose preparing us for labor, and labor for repose. In the Lord's prayer, the clause, "THY WILL BE DONE," has in all ages received a double interpretation; as being either a prayer for all men, that they may obey God; or as being an act of personal submission. Probably it includes both meanings; and so the Christian, in every moment of his Christian life, may unite the sense of responsibility and the sense of dependence, obedience, and love. His *aim* is, by his every act and his total influence, to advance the kingdom of Christ; but to do this by becoming, in every act, and in his total influence, the organ by which Christ shall act, the channel through which Christ's influence shall flow.

§ 62 The Evil of Cultivating exclusively the Goodness of Effort.

Now, what is the harm of aiming exclusively or chiefly at *working out our own salvation*, that is, of cultivating exclusively the goodness of Intention or Effort?

The first evil is, that we are led to look at ourselves, instead of looking at God. Our own duties, our own responsibilities, our own sins, our own virtues, fill our mind. There is nothing in the sight of these things to animate us; all are discouraging and gloomy subjects of thought. They shut us up in a very narrow circle. They produce a morbid anxiety about our condition; a spiritual hypochondria. They produce a refined selfishness. We become the centre and pivot of all transactions and events; we are of the greatest consequence in our own eyes; we are perpetually contemplating ourselves. There is a spiritual egotism, and a religious selfishness, which is almost as bad as the selfishness of the worldling. To think of our own soul continually is perhaps better than not to think of it at all, but only somewhat better.

Again: By aiming exclusively at working for God and earning our own salvation, we accustom ourselves to regard God in one of his attributes exclusively, — that of Justice. He becomes to us an inexorable Law; and an inexorable Law is only a little better than a merciless Fate. This is the great evil of Calvinism. It sees God as Law, and not as Love; it regards all goodness as in the motive, none as in the character. It cannot recognize goodness as beauty: it recognizes it only as intention. But what an immense injury is it to the human heart to see God habitually as a Judge, and not as a Father! For all the best affections are frozen at their source, when we fail to see that his essential Being is based in Love, — free, unlimited, ever-active Love. But not only Calvinism, but also its opposite, Unitarianism, often fails in this same point. The idea of Justice eclipses that of Love in the view of both systems. Both tend to separate from God, and to destroy the habit of filial affection, by seeing him too exclusively as the supporter of a Moral Order, and the avenger of the broken law.

For these and other reasons, we see that the effort to do right does not necessarily lead to the happy, spontaneous, and loving practice of goodness. This is to be found, not in the Law, but in the Gospel; not in the sight of Duty, but in the sight of Love. It is affectionate, filial gratitude for unbought, unearned mercy. It is the great love of him who has been forgiven much. It is the overflowing affection of the Prodigal, whose Father has received him on his return, not with severity, but with rejoicing. It comes from the sight of the infinite beauty scattered through the world, the blessed face of nature, the warm and glowing heart of humanity, the infinite adaptations throughout the universe for the comfort, education, and blessing of God's creatures. To look out of ourselves and away from ourselves; away from our narrow virtues and our small attainments; away from our dangers, our sinfulness, our folly; to look wholly away from ourselves, and to gaze constantly at the fulness of beauty and goodness in the creation and providence of God, — will not this touch the cold heart, and moisten the dry eye, with an humble and grateful tear? "If," says a recent author, "if, for every rebuke we utter of men's vices, we put forth a claim upon their hearts; if, for every assertion of God's demands from them, we could substitute a display of his kindness to them; if, side by side with every warning of death, we could exhibit proofs and promises of immortality; if, in fine, instead of assuming the being of an awful Deity, which men, though they cannot and dare not deny, are always unwilling, sometimes unable, to conceive, we were to show them a near, visible, inevitable, but all-beneficent Deity, whose presence makes the earth itself a heaven, I think there would be fewer deaf children sitting in the market-place."

§ 63. Forgiveness the Practical Solution of the Problem of Evil.

The Doctrine of Forgiveness, as stated in this essay, is the practical solution of the great problem of moral evil. The question, " How can the existence of evil be reconciled with the perfections of the Deity?" is a question to which no intellectual theory can furnish any adequate reply. Every Theodicee, from that of Leibnitz to the last Essay on Moral Evil in our theological journals, makes out its explanation, either by explaining away the Reality of Evil, or by explaining away the Perfections of the Deity. But, though no speculative solution of this problem can be offered to the intellect, a practical solution is offered to the moral nature in the doctrine of forgiven sin. For sin, when forgiven, produces a deeper and more ardent love to God than would have existed if there had been no sin. As charcoal, the darkest substance in nature, is the basis of the diamond, which is the most brilliant; so Sin is the base and dark material which, by the power of God's forgiving love, is transformed into the brightest jewel of the Heavenly World. Sin thus becomes the occasion of developing a divine perfection which otherwise would never have been known, and a human virtue which without it would never have existed. This is no answer to the speculative difficulty; for the inquiry may always still be made, "Why could not the same end have been reached by a perfect being in some other way?" But the heart which perceives that by this mysterious alchemy all its evil has been swallowed up in good, and its sins made the Substance of holiness, can rest well satisfied here. The difficulty which perplexed the heart is gone, and there only remain admiring Wonder and grateful Joy.

§ 64. And of the Problem of Human Freedom and Divine Providence

And the Doctrine of Grace, of which the Doctrine of Forgiveness is a part, contains also the practical solution of the problem of the Divine Providence as in conflict with Human Freedom. This problem also arises from the fact that man's mind can see at once truths of eternity and facts of time, and is therefore incapable of speculative solution. Every attempt must fail; because, as finite beings, we cannot comprehend that which, as connected with the infinite world, we are able to see and know. Therefore, all attempts at a theoretical solution of the difficulty end either in denying the Divine Providence, or in denying the Freedom of man. But the practical solution is obtained, when we perceive that while man is allowed freely to choose evil, and to obey unrighteousness, the Divine purpose, which is his sanctification and redemption, is obtained at last even by means of that very unrighteousness and evil.

The Divine Providence which chooses man for goodness before the foundation of the world, and determines his happiness, is magnified when we see how all paths, however circuitous, tend to the same end. In every moment of time, man is free by nature to obey or to disobey; to choose the right or the wrong; to go toward God or from Him. But, while the right choice brings the soul immediately and directly to God, the wrong choice tends the same way, though mediately and indirectly. The circling line, sooner or later, must return into itself. And our natural freedom consists in being able indefinitely, but not infinitely, to enlarge the circle, and postpone its return. In the fact of forgiven sin we discover the returning bend of the circle, and see the certainty of the apostolic declaration, that "Every knee shall bow," and that "*in the dispensation of the fulness of times* God will gather in one all things in Christ, in heaven and on earth." But this Divine Decree, in its triumph, also exalts human freedom by changing natural liberty (which is only the power of choice) into spiritual liberty, which includes both choice and action. The glorious liberty of the sons of God is the liberty both to will and to do of his good pleasure. It is the fulness of life, — the harmonious activity of all the powers of the soul, which no longer, by mutual conflict, check and restrain each other. It is the change of *wilfulness*, which is as the freedom of the bird pecking at the bars of its cage, into the will, made free by the power of truth and the law of liberty, — which is like the unhindered flight of the eagle, who sails with supreme dominion through the depths of air, in a direct course to his everlasting mountain-home.

§ 65. Conclusion.

We have thus completed our survey of the doctrine of Forgiveness. We first showed how important a position it occupies in the New Testament and in Christian experience.

We next pointed out the difficulties arising from the fact, that it appeared to contradict the doctrine of Retribution; a doctrine which, as we saw, also holds a most important place in the New Testament and in Christian experience. We then attempted to reconcile this contradiction, and to show that these two great doctrines were not contradictory, but antagonist; and that on the basis of this very antagonism depends the higher life of the soul. We showed that God reveals himself on one side as Law, and on the other side as Love; and that the sight of Law and Love are both necessary for the Christian Life, — the sight of law awakening the sense of responsibility, and the sight of love awakening the sense of dependence. We showed the place of faith and of works, of activity and receptivity, of energetic obedience and quiet waiting, in the Christian Life. After this we considered the objections to the doctrine of forgiveness; saw how far it was a work of God, of Christ, of man, and of the

Church; and lastly, considered the nature of the New Life flowing out of it. And now it would be profitable, had we space in this essay, to consider at length the History of the Doctrine. We should find in the Sacrifices, Priesthood, and Ritual of all religions, how deeply such a doctrine is needed by the human soul, — reading in all these the confession, that man feels himself estranged from God by sin, and is always seeking for some mode of Reconciliation. We should see this need fully expressed, but only partially relieved, by the Sacrifices and Ritual of the Jewish law, which were a shadow of good things to come, but which did not fully relieve the conscience, or take away the sense of sin (Heb. x. 2). Yet even in Judaism we should see how much of ardent piety and holy effort resulted from the partial manifestation made of God's pardoning mercy by means of that ritual. In the life of Jesus we should find the full manifestation of Divine Grace; we should see therein a love irrespective of the merit of its object; a love which makes no condition, except that its offers should be accepted; a love proportioned, not to the deserts, but to the necessities, of man. In the epistles of Paul we should find the first doctrinal statement of this great fact, and this doctrinal statement made the central point of his Doctrinal System. By this doctrine of Grace, Paul brought the Gentile world to the feet of Jesus, and planted in Europe the Seeds of all our spiritual and moral culture, and of all Modern Civilization, Literature, Art, and Science. This doctrine of Grace, having been lost sight of, was revived by the great Aurelius Augustine at the end of the Fourth Century. His soul of fire, penetrated to its lowest depths by the living conviction of God's free love, gave a new and vast impulse to the human mind. But it is the nature of our human life to allow the forms in which a creative spirit has embodied itself finally to cover, conceal, and destroy the spirit itself. The vital impulse given by such

RESULTS OF FORGIVENESS. 163

men as Paul and Augustine embodies itself in institutions; expresses itself by symbolic ceremonies, and a rich worship; excites a vast amount of laborious outward activity; speaks in words of burning force and sharpest precision; and then the spirit which has produced all this is lost sight of in the reverence paid to its own work. Then men reverence forms, ceremonies, creeds, outward institutions; and seek to be saved by a pedantic observation of this routine of works, rather than by the faith which first produced them. So it was that the doctrines of Grace first taught by Paul, then lost sight of and revived by Augustine, were once more lost sight of, and again revived by Luther. The doctrine of justification by faith, proclaimed by Luther, was the vital principle of the reformation of the Sixteenth Century, and again became a new impulse of life to the human race. Its negative work, its work of denial, conflict, and overthrow, is easily seen and measured; but the positive result of

Luther's Reformation was faith in the unbought love of God to the human soul; and there is no modern reform, nothing which diffuses comfort, intelligence, power, among the millions, but may be traced to this great spiritual movement of the Sixteenth Century. But now, standing in the midst of the Nineteenth Century, we may ask, "IS NOT A NEW REVIVAL OF THIS GREAT DOCTRINE NEEDED BY THE CHURCH AND BY THE WORLD?" Have not the works of the reformation once more eclipsed its interior principle? One party supposes that the essential principle of the reformation consists in the creeds and opinions held by the Reformers; and another party supposes that it consists in their assertion of the Sufficiency of the Scriptures, and the Right of Private Judgment. Consequently we have a new idolatry of forms; and we worship, in our day, Creeds, the Letter of the Bible, and self-formed Opinions. And so again we cut ourselves off from the current of that inspiring Life which creates creeds, scriptures, and opinions, but is never created by them. Once more we need to go behind all these works of our own hands and minds, back to God's free love, which can again make all things new. As, when the Holy Spirit descended on the day of Pentecost, a rushing and mighty wind filled all the house where they were sitting; so the houses of doctrine and form must be filled by a new inspiration, and God once more shake not the Earth only, but the Heavens; not the world only, but the Church. The new Revival of the doctrine of Grace will by no means express itself in the old language; for each age has a new form of application for the same truth. The language of Luther differed from that of Augustine. The language of Augustine differed from that of Paul. The human race repeats evermore the same experiences, and passes through the same errors; yet the truth each time is attained in a larger and higher form. The human race does not revolve in a circle, but ascends in a spiral;

passing, indeed, again and again through the same errors to the same truths, but passing through them each time on a higher plane. Thus, though no man can predict what form the doctrines of Grace will take in that new manifestation for which our century is waiting, we may be sure that such a manifestation must come. And among its negative results we may expect to see the destruction of Sectarian ramparts, the breaking down of narrow Creeds, the overthrow of a merely polemic Theology, and a merely ecclesiastic Ritual; while among its positive results we may expect the foundation of a new Church collected out of all sects under heaven; a Church not of the Priesthood nor the Clergy, but of the PEOPLE, whose ritual shall consist of action as well as of prayer, of humanity as well as piety; and the central points of whose creed shall be, that GOD IS THE UNIVERSAL FATHER AND THAT ALL MANKIND ARE BRETHREN.

THE END.

www.ingramcontent.com/pod-product-compliance
Lightning Source LLC
Chambersburg PA
CBHW051104160426
43193CB00010B/1309